# PATHWAYS FROM HEROIN ADDICTION
# RECOVERY WITHOUT TREATMENT

Health, Society, and Policy, a series edited by
Sheryl Ruzek and Irving Kenneth Zola

Temple University Press   Philadelphia

# PATHWAYS FROM HEROIN ADDICTION

## RECOVERY WITHOUT TREATMENT

Patrick Biernacki

Temple University Press, Philadelphia 19122
© 1986 by Temple University. All rights reserved
Published 1986
Printed in the United States of America

**Library of Congress Cataloging-in-Publication Data**

Biernacki, Patrick, 1941–
Pathways from heroin addiction.
(Health, society, and policy)
Bibliography: p. 233
Includes index
1. Heroin Dependence—rehabilitation.   WM 288 B588p]
HV5822.H4B54   1986        36.2′93        85-22283
ISBN 0-87722-410-2
HV5822.H4B54   1986        36.2′93        85-22283
ISBN 0-87722-410-2

The book's epigraph is from *The Last Connection: A Story About Heroin Told by Ali Baba to Edward Rose.*
Boulder, Colo.: Waiting Room Press, 1980, pp. 92–93.
It is used here with the permission of Edward Rose.

As I said,
if you want to stop,
there has to be something
        to replace the habit,
something that brings any sense
        into your life,
to make you able to forget
        about scag.

For me it was at first
the thought of—of me being able to—
to be happy without—or
to get fun out of life,
        nice feelings, good vibrations,
without it—the thought of it or
the knowing, the knowledge,

and finally and for the most part
having a kid,
        because this is—

You know,
it makes me seeing
the sense of life
in the most direct way.

R:   Having a kid, that doesn't help drunkards.
A:   Well, maybe it doesn't help junkies, but it did help me.

When—When I had—When I felt the
feeling of responsibility for my kid,
it made me able to feel responsible
        for myself again.
Therefore right now I couldn't imagine
myself being a junky
        for the next time.
If feel the responsibility
        for myself again.

I have my son.
For the street junkies belonging to that scene,
        it's of importance because
it's the last human connection at all they got,
        yes, with any—any people.
                Besides that
they are just by themselves
looking right into the eyes
        of death.

That's the last connection.
                    —Edward Rose

For Catherine Zepka

*Who did not drop me in the coalbin*

# Contents

# Preface

In this book I analyze how some illicit opiate addicts have overcome their addiction and "recovered"[1] on their own, without benefit of professional help or therapeutic regimen. Since opiate addiction generally is believed to be one of the most powerful forms of addiction, the idea that people can quit using opiates on their own, or "naturally" as I have termed it in this book, is likely to stir some controversy. Given this possibility, it is essential to state clearly at the outset my intentions with this work.

In no way do I mean to imply, or wish to be interpreted by others as advocating or suggesting, that people experiment with opiates. Experimentation with opiates, especially under current conditions in the United States, is a perilous undertaking. The possession of opiate drugs is illegal, and their use outside medical situations is condemned. The physical properties of these drugs also present a number of serious dangers, including the possibility of death from an overdose. In addition, although this book concerns how people, through their own initiative, can overcome an addiction to opiates, I must emphasize that, for most people, the course of natural recovery is very difficult to complete. Finally, my analysis should not be taken to mean that if all drug addicts were left alone, they would eventually stop using drugs of their own accord. Addicts differ greatly in their personal and

1. Throughout this book, I use such words as "recovered" and "cured" guardedly. I do not wish to imply that the fact of opiate addiction necessarily means that a person so addicted is sick or ill.

social resources, and many addicts who wish to break their bond with the drug could, in this regard, benefit from professional intervention.

Since the 1920s, a social problems perspective has held sway over the field of drug research and treatment. Opiate addiction has been perceived as a serious problem that has to be controlled, if not totally eradicated. Since the 1960s, research efforts have concentrated on documenting how people become addicted, on the incidence of addiction, and on how addicts might best be treated. This perspective has turned research efforts away from developing a more thorough substantive understanding of the natural course of addiction as it might unfold to its termination. My overall intention in writing this book is to take up the gap by providing some understanding, however incomplete, of the natural processes that culminate in ending an addiction to opiate drugs. Within this framework, my foremost goal is to provide an objective but still empathetic account and analysis of the courses of natural recovery that I found. By adding to the knowledge in this area I can imagine possible benefits for a number of audiences, including those concerned with issues of social policy, clinicians, the lay community, and, it is to be hoped, drug addicts.

Understanding how self-initiated, natural recovery occurs could help in the formulation of more thoughtful social policies concerning illicit drug use and addiction. Clinicians also might benefit, in that the analysis could enable them to recognize better the various needs of addicts who want to stop their drug use and assist them in fashioning specific therapeutic techniques to meet those needs. Members of the lay community (and indirectly, the addicts in the community) could benefit from the information in this book because it might change their attitudes and sensitivities concerning addiction and thus, perhaps, better enable them to deal with the problem. Finally, by empirically and analytically confronting the proverbial belief that "once an addict, always an addict," people who are addicted to opiates might learn how self-defeating the notion is and eventually understand that, should they be inclined to do so, they might be able to discontinue their drug use on their own.

Some of the materials in this book, particularly sections in Chapter 2 and Appendix A, were published elsewhere and were co-authored with Dan Waldorf. In most instances, however, these earlier publications presented only preliminary analyses and limited descriptions. When replications of earlier materials appear in this book, they do so with greater specificity and elaboration than was possible before.

The interviews that provide the substance for the book were conducted between August 1978 and June 1980. The respondents had stopped their addictive use of opiates for at least two years before they were interviewed; the range in the length of time they had stopped was between two and twenty-six years. The respondents were addicted at some point between 1952 and 1978. In terms of social policy, this period is not different from the current situation. Social policy still is one of prohibition and control of opiate drugs and the voluntary or involuntary treatment of addicts.

My exposition of the social-psychological processes that culminate in the recovery from opiate addiction without the aid of any professional intervention takes a rather linear course. In the introductory chapter I create a backdrop for the problem to be addressed—how people can recover from opiate addiction on their own—and I describe the conceptual approach that frames and guides my analysis. I try in the analysis faithfully to "ground" the conceptualizations and arguments in materials that the respondents provided and to tell their stories, as much as possible, from their points of view (Glaser 1978; Glaser and Strauss 1967).

In the second chapter I discuss the situations that arise among addicts that give them the impetus to stop using opiate drugs and how they formulate resolutions to change their lives. The third chapter centers on the problems that addicts confront when they attempt to carry out their resolutions to stop using drugs and the strategies and techniques they employ to solve them and break away from the world of addiction. Chapter 4 focuses on the problems entailed in remaining abstinent once the state initially is accomplished. I devote particular attention here to examining the "craving phenomenon" and the methods that successfully abstaining individuals utilize to manage and overcome the experience. In Chapter 5 I provide the final substantive part of the analysis, the social and subjective processes of transforming the prior "deviant" identities of the addict into an array of "ordinary" ones. That is, I analyze and discuss the various courses through which people who once were addicted can and do develop a new arrangement of ordinary identities wherein the addict identity and corresponding perspective are either excluded or greatly deemphasized. In the concluding chapter I try to condense all the materials, conceptualizations, and arguments that I have presented concerning the natural recovery from opiate addiction into a concise statement; I also point out some of the social policy implications and shortcomings of my work.

A methodological chapter appears as Appendix A. Among other things, it explains and analyzes how the study respondents were found and the efforts that were taken to ensure the validity of the information they provided. The interview guide for the tape-recorded sessions appears as Appendix B. Appendix C lists certain major characteristics of individual respondents, among them age, race, and years of addiction. No judgments are made, or should be made, about these charts; they are offered for informational purposes only.

# Acknowledgments

I am indebted to many people. First, I am beholden to those officers at the National Institute on Drug Abuse who believed the research was worthwhile and funded the project as Grant #1–H81–DA–01988. I owe a particular debt to Dr. Frank Tims, the project staff officer. He encouraged me, helped ease my way through the institutional forms and regulations, and thereby facilitated the project's completion. A large debt also is due the project staff, especially Dan Waldorf, the study's co-principal investigator, who played an essential role in managing the project and helping to collect the research data.

A number of people worked on the project in different but equally important capacities. Eddie Washington and James Jorquez helped locate people to study, conducted interviews, and made some contributions to the analysis. Shelia Murphy, Genny Buehler, and Ann Wettrich also did some interviewing; in addition, Genny and Ann completed the excruciating task of transcribing the hundreds of hours of tape-recorded interviews into typescript.

Appreciation also is due the Pacific Institute for Research and Evaluation, a nonprofit corporation in Lafayette, California. The institute managed the project's financing and offered additional forms of support whenever it was needed. I thank Setsu Gee, executive director of the Institute for Scientific Analysis in San Francisco, another nonprofit research corporation, for her effort in shepherding the manuscript through its many drafts and revisions. I also thank Jean Ross for typing one draft of the manuscript. Michael Jang, also with ISA, programmed and computer-processed the study's quantitative data.

The project was situated in the offices of the Prisoner's Union in San Francisco. The Union, a prison reform group that represents the rights of felons, helped to legitimize the research in the community. Union staff were extremely helpful; staff members patiently tolerated us through several disruptive and troublesome moments during the research.

A number of people read earlier drafts of this book, or parts of it, and offered thoughtful comments that helped to shape its present content and form. I wish to extend special thanks here to Ann Biernacki, Robert Broadhead, Kathy Charmaz, Harvey Feldman, Lyn Lofland, Jerry Mandel, Anselm Strauss, and the editors of the series, Irving Zola and Sheryl Ruzek. I thank them for their generous support and specific commentary.

Finally, this book would have been impossible without the cooperation of the people who participated in the study and who must remain nameless. For some of them, the interviews proved to be a disturbing experience during which they relived painful parts of their pasts. I hope the final product justifies any hardship they might have endured as a result of helping me to complete this work.

**Pathways from Heroin Addiction**
**Recovery Without Treatment**

# 1

## Reappraising Recovery Models

Scott is a 42-year-old man.[1] He is remarkably youthful in appearance, considering the fact that he was once a dope addict. Through an eleven-year period, Scott took a large variety of illicit drugs. He had a great number of psychedelic "trips" on LSD, had an eighteen-month "run" on methamphetamines, and was addicted to heroin for more than four years.

Scott was raised in a middle-class family. He had a happy childhood and a normal adolescence; nothing terribly traumatic happened to him, and he was not a delinquent. During his high school years he experimented with alcohol and marijuana, but he did not use heroin until he was 21 years old and in college. Recalling his first experience with heroin, he said, "I liked it right off." Thereafter, he used it as often as he could, but he did not become addicted to the drug until later. Scott was a good student, and after he received his bachelor's degree he moved to another city and began graduate school.

In 1967 Scott was studying for a master's degree. It was the time of Haight-Ashbury, Flower Children, and psyche-

---

1. Although this abbreviated account, and the others I present in this book, are true, the names used and other possible identifying characteristics have been changed or deleted to preserve the anonymity of the people involved. Otherwise, all the firsthand reports appear as they were told, without alteration. The numbers in parenthesis after interviews and quoted material refer to the study respondents who are listed in Appendix C.

delic drugs. Scott discovered LSD and used it extensively. He also continued to use heroin, on occasion, when it was available.

Scott finished his graduate studies and went to work for a social service agency. When he was 26, he fell in love and married. He affectionately remembered this period as being quite romantic. However, he continued to take drugs. For more than a year, he took methamphetamines almost daily. He also used heroin sporadically. At the same time he led a rather conventional life—he wanted to have a family, he continued to work, he paid his bills, and he bought a house.

Scott's wife began using heroin with him. At first they restricted their use to weekends, but he soon found he was injecting the drug on Monday mornings so that he could go to work. In a short time he was using on a daily basis. Over the next year or so, he and his wife maintained a pattern of using heroin each day for a few weeks and then withdrawing on a weekend, only to start again the following week. Scott claimed that his addiction did not interfere with his work, although he did admit that he did not function as well as he should have. Somehow, he recalled, he "managed through it."

Shortly after Scott was married, his relationship with his wife became very cool and distant. The romance was gone. Scott did not think that their drug use contributed to the problem, and for a period he continued to make a go of the marriage. For a long time, both husband and wife were very depressed; finally, on the spur of the moment, he moved out of the house and into a hotel. Scott harbored the hope that the breakup was temporary, but things did not improve. His wife stayed in their house and stopped using drugs, while Scott lived alone in a hotel. He was depressed, thought about committing suicide, and kept on using heroin. Later in his life, he thought that the heroin helped him get through this difficult period.

For more than four years, Scott was addicted to heroin, yet he continued to work at the same job. His source for the drug was very stable, and aside from those times when he had to purchase the drug, he rarely associated with other addicts. In fact, the lifestyle of street addicts—the hustling, the distrust, the meanness—frightened him.

Scott largely supported his addiction in a manner consistent with his middle-class lifestyle. When his paycheck did not provide enough money to pay for the drugs he needed, he would obtain a bank loan, borrow money from his credit union, or borrow on his credit cards. One time he cashed some stolen payroll checks, but this was unusual. Occasionally, it was necessary to shut himself in his hotel room, withdraw from the drug, and resume using it later. Scott claimed that he never borrowed or stole money from his family or friends.

Eventually, Scott's financial resources ran out, and he realized he had gone as far as he possibly could go. He could not "manage it anymore in terms of work, money, and dope." He knew "the only way [he] was going to be able to manage it was to start dealing drugs, and [he] didn't want to take the chance of getting busted." He recalled: "It finally became clear that this was the end. If I was going to keep using dope, I was going to have to make a big change, and start dealing. I wasn't willing to make that change because I didn't think it would work. It was a rational decision to stop."

Once again, Scott shut himself in his hotel room and withdrew from the heroin. This time, however, it was different—he did not resume his old pattern and start using again. Within a few weeks of the point at which he stopped, he began to visit with old friends and started to spend a lot of time socializing with them. About a year later, he moved back with his wife. They had a child, but the renewed relationship did not work out, and they finally divorced.

Scott used heroin over a period of eleven years. He worked at the same job for more than sixteen years, during four of which he was addicted. Scott never was arrested and did not sell drugs or hustle very much when he was addicted. Scott never received any kind of professional or clinical treatment for his addiction, yet he has not returned to using heroin for ten years. He has remarried, is still working at the same job, and does not use any illicit drugs. (071)

How could this happen? Scott's experiences run against most of our common understandings concerning opiate addicts and addiction. Although he did have some problems, he did not become dissolute or wantonly criminal. He maintained a relatively conventional lifestyle, and what is most significant, he successfully stopped using heroin on his own without the aid of any therapeutic intervention.

Accepted notions would have us believe that once people become addicted to opiate drugs, they will always be addicted to them. Somehow, the bond developed to the addictive drug is believed to be everlasting—it is a tie so strong that once it is knotted, it cannot freely be dissolved or voluntarily broken. "Till death do us part" aptly describes most conventional beliefs about opiate addiction.

What substance, then, do these widely shared conceptions about addiction really have? Since opiates were introduced into the United States more than two centuries ago, millions of people have used them, and more than tens of thousands have become addicted to them (Brecher 1972). Are we to conclude that, without therapeutic intervention, all these people were destined to remain addicted for their entire lives? Or is it possible that many of them, like Scott, came to a point where they voluntarily stopped using and recovered on their own—what I term a "natural" recovery? The materials and analyses I present in this book explore this latter possibility and seriously challenge the widely accepted belief that "once an addict, always an addict."

To discover empirically how a recovery from opiate addiction can be achieved "naturally," the research study on which this book is based was designed to locate and interview people who stopped using opiates without professional intervention or any therapeutic regimen. The experiences of locating people who had stopped, and the analysis of the life-history materials gathered from interviews with them, led to the following conclusions:

· Addicts can and do recover "naturally"—on their own without the aid of any therapeutic intervention.
· Naturally recovered former addicts are relatively easy to find and interview.
· Addicts are not alike in character or lifestyle.
· All addicts do not undergo the same social careers or become equally affected by their addiction.
· Some addicts lead basically "straight" lives, that is, they are not criminals.
· Some addicts manage to isolate their addiction from their involvements in other social worlds.
· Some people drift in and out of their addiction without much conscious thought or consideration.
· Some addicts can and do overcome cravings to use opiates when they are abstinent and thereby avoid relapsing.
· Addict folklore and professional understandings do not adequately explain those addicts who have quit on their own.
· Some people who have stopped their addiction to opiates do not continue to think of themselves as addicted.

These findings are discussed in detail in this book. The

remainder of this chapter discusses prevailing theories on addiction as well as the theoretical framework and the methods used in this research.

## Physiological Aspects of Opiate Addiction

### Opiate Drugs

When I use the term *opiate drugs*, I mean to include opium and its derivatives—morphine, heroin, dilaudid, and codeine—as well as synthetically similar drugs such as demerol and methadone. These narcotic drugs are used legitimately for a variety of medical purposes. They work primarily through the central nervous system and commonly are prescribed to relieve pain, to induce sedation and sleep, to suppress chronic coughing, and to relieve diarrhea. Although narcotics are known to have these physiological effects, they also have concomitant side effects that are experienced subjectively and are described differently by the people who use them. Some people who have used narcotics, even in medical settings, complain of feeling nauseated and anxious, and have defined the overall experience as very unpleasant. Others have defined the general experience as quite pleasant; they feel content or even euphoric. (For a fuller discussion of the physiological effects of narcotic drugs, see Jaffe 1970.)

### Drug Tolerance and Dependence

In spite of the obvious beneficial uses of narcotics, their use presents certain dangers. One significant danger, in addition to the possibility of death from an overdose, results from the chemical properties of opiates, which can produce a physiological dependency if they are used on a regular, daily basis over time. People who habitually use opiate drugs can develop a tolerance to them; when this happens, they have to take increasingly larger amounts of the drug to obtain the same initial effects. Tolerance develops as the body becomes progressively immune to the chemical effects of the drug at the cellular level. Should usage continue, a physiological dependence on the narcotic will occur as the affected tissues and cells accommodate the chemically induced processes that result from the introduction of the drug. The homeostatic processes of the body adjust to the narcotic and bring about a new physiological equilibrium. If the equilibrium and normal functioning are to be maintained, at the physiological level, regular and stable amounts of the drug must be taken. Narcotic drugs also have a "cross-tolerance." This means that a person dependent on one drug—say, heroin—can take an equivalent dosage of a similar drug—for example, morphine—and maintain the existing equilibrium of the body.

Once a physiological dependence on narcotic drugs is established, maintenance doses of the drug must be taken or the drug-accommodated equilibrium will be upset and symptoms of drug withdrawal will appear. Withdrawal symptoms will be experienced until the physiological processes readjust and bring about a narcotic-free state of equilibrium.[2] Physical addiction is usually thought of as the state where a tolerance to a narcotic drug has developed to the extent that the person is dependent, and uncomfortable physical symptoms appear in the absence of the drug. It should be emphasized that addiction does not result from a single administration of the drug; many people have used illicit narcotics for years on an occasional basis without becoming addicted to them (Zinberg and Jacobson 1976).

Keys to understanding the nature of opiate addiction and

2. This is a rather simple description of the phenomena of drug tolerance and dependence. A more complete discussion of the complexities and puzzling aspects of these processes can be found in Cochlin 1974.

the behavior of addicts are the conditions of drug tolerance and dependence (especially as they are manifested to the user through the physiological symptoms of withdrawal). The tolerance that results with the continued, regular use of the drug often is posited as responsible for a great deal of addict behavior, particularly the stereotypic criminal behavior commonly associated with illicit street addicts. That is, with regular use, for the opiate to be effective (e.g., to relieve pain in a medical situation or induce euphoria in a non-medical setting), the amount of the drug used must progressively be increased beyond the level of tolerance that has developed. Thus, if maintenance is not the goal, increasing amounts of the drug are needed to bring about the desired effect. Conversely, if withdrawal symptoms are to be avoided, equivalent amounts of the addictive drug must be taken at regular intervals.

*Withdrawal Symptoms*

A person who has developed a physiological dependence on opiates will become ill if regular administrations suddenly cease. Characteristic symptoms of withdrawal usually begin to appear within ten to twelve hours following the last use of the drug. Although the symptoms are highly variable, typical signs of opiate withdrawal include restlessness, irritability, insomnia, involuntary twitching of the muscles, muscle pain (especially in the back and legs), sweating and flushed skin, runny nose and eyes, chills, stomach cramps, nausea, vomiting, loss of appetite, and diarrhea. Some people who have withdrawn from opiates "cold turkey" have equated the experience to having a severe case of the flu. I should emphasize, however, that the severity of withdrawal is variable and is related to subjective factors as well as to the general health of the person and, especially, to the size of the habit and the quality of the drug used. Usually, the physical symptoms reach their most severe point forty-eight to seventy-two hours after the drug was last used; then they begin to abate. (Of course, the symptoms can be dispelled quickly by administering an opiate drug.)

*Relapse*

A successful withdrawal from opiates and the overcoming of the physical dependence do not necessarily resolve the problem of addiction. Conventional understanding and much research evidence would have us believe that people who withdraw from opiate drugs have an almost unalterable tendency to start using opiates again and become readdicted, even after long periods of abstinence. For example, many follow-up studies of drug treatment programs are consistent in showing that the great majority of addicted people (sometimes as many as 80 to 90 percent) who go through these programs relapse and return to using narcotics in a short time following their release or discharge (Hunt and Odoroff 1962; Stephens and Cottrell 1972). Evidence of this kind adds substance to the "once an addict, always an addict" belief. Some of these findings are misleading, however; other research has shown that people who have been addicted can withdraw from the drug and voluntarily abstain from further use (Graeven and Graeven 1983; Waldorf and Biernacki 1979; Winick 1962). In any event, the tendency of some people to relapse and become readdicted, often after long periods of abstinence, is a perplexing aspect of addiction and a feature that should be addressed in any theory attempting to explain it.

**Theories of Addiction and Possibilities of Recovery**

As is true for other kinds of disruptive human behavior that have come to the attention of scientists (e.g., alcoholism or delinquency), there are almost as many theories about drug

addiction as there are perspectives on it. When dealing with
behavioral issues, in many instances the "scientific" understandings parallel those held in the lay community and reflect conventional stereotypes and existing cultural images
of the behavior in question.[3] Some "scientific" or clinical
theories also implicitly take distinct moral positions concerning the behavior in question.[4] Finally, most theories at
least suggest an approach to ameliorate the condition and/or
treat the problematic behavior. As a comparative backdrop
for my analysis of the processes of opiate addiction and
recovery, I first provide a brief description of some major,
competing theories concerning the phenomenon. My discussion of these theories is organized on the basis of the primary perspective of each theory—whether it is primarily
biochemical, psychological, sociological, or social-psychological.

## Biochemical Theories

Generally speaking, biochemical theories propose that opiate addiction results from preexisting (possibly inherited)
physiological deficiencies or from specific alterations in the
body's metabolism brought on by exposure to opiate drugs
(Dole and Nyswander 1967; Goldstein 1976; Jones and Jones
1977). Typical of biochemical theories is one that has to do
with the recent discovery of a group of biochemical agents
called *endorphins*. These substances are produced in the
human body and resemble morphine in their structure and
effect. Under normal conditions they are hypothesized to
enter the receptor sites of particular cells that have been

---

3. A more systematic and detailed analysis of the relationship between
scientific theorizing and conventional understandings in the area of drug addiction can be found in Movahedi 1978.
4. For a more thorough review and critique of contemporary theories of
addiction, see Alexander and Hadaway 1981.

activated to receive them and function to relieve pain and stress. According to the biochemical theory supporting this view, addiction would result either from a genetically determined endorphin deficiency or from a temporary or permanent impairment of the body's ability to produce endorphins due to the external intake of heroin or some other opiate (Restak 1977). Because of the deficiency of naturally produced endorphins, an abstaining addict would, for example, be unusually sensitive to feelings of pain or stress and thus would be inclined once again to use narcotic drugs and possibly become readdicted.

From the biochemical view, the addict is a sick person in the sense that the body is malfunctioning. Treatment entails measures to "correct" the physiological deficiency, perhaps through the provision of a supplementary chemical regimen such as methadone (a synthetic, morphine-like analgesic) or heroin. The maintenance regimen takes up the endorphin deficiency, prevents the onset of withdrawal symptoms, and thereby removes the need to use other opiates.

Biochemical theories are rather deterministic and somewhat unclear in their prognosis concerning people who are in programs like methadone maintenance. That is, it is uncertain whether the physiological deficiency can eventually be corrected or whether those people who are on a maintenance regimen will have to remain on it for their entire lives.[5]

### Psychological Theories

Like biochemical theories, most theories from the psychological perspective place responsibility for addiction with the individual. Psychological theories differ from biochemi-

---

5. For a far-reaching critique of methadone maintenance programs, see Nelkin 1973.

cal ones, however, in that the "cause" of the behavior is located in the personalities of addicts, not in their physical bodies. Addicts are seen as weak-willed people, emotionally immature, morally deficient, or, more generally, as people afflicted with "personality" or "character" disorders (Chein and Rosenfeld 1957; Rado 1933). Often these theories reflect many common-sense, stereotypic notions about addicts and addiction (Movahedi 1978).

From the psychological perspective, the addict is considered to be a particular "kind" of person, for example, an addict is a person with an "addictive personality." Here, addiction is seen as stemming from immaturity and a corresponding lack of willpower. The immature person seeks immediate pleasure and gratification and cannot resist temptations to use the addictive drug. Moreover, the lifestyle of the illicit street addict is seen as being particularly well suited to these "kinds" of people because it provides them with a sense of identity and a social niche that makes few demands on them.[6] Psychological theories posit that the personality deficits of addicts originate in problematic family relations during childhood—for example, from the absence of "good" role models, from contradictory parental expectations, or from a lack of love and respect.

Psychological theories are almost absolute in their perspective. Since the addict is viewed as a "kind" of person, then the addictive behavior (or some other, equally unwanted behavior, such as alcoholism) will persist until a form of therapeutic intervention takes place and the person is changed. Very simply, addicts are "sick" people and require help. The immediate source of the addictive behavior is the personality, which first must be changed or "corrected" if the addiction is to be cured. Addicts who attempt to abstain on their own

6. A contrary view of the street addict can be found in Preble and Casey 1969.

are doomed to relapse unless the underlying problems—personality deficits—are corrected.

## Sociological Theories

In contrast to biochemical and psychological theories about addiction, sociological theories typically propose that the conditions of despair, frustration, and hopelessness, and the general feeling of alienation suffered by many disadvantaged segments of our society, are primarily responsible for addiction and for relapse among addicts who are attempting to abstain. For example, minority youth living in city slums or barrios may come to feel that their situation is hopeless, that they have no chance of getting ahead. Under these conditions, they may try to adapt to their perceived situation through a "retreatist" form of behavior—drug addiction—characterized by a rejection of both those things that are valued by society and the accepted ways to attain them (Merton 1957).

One variation on this view considers addicts to be "double failures," persons who have failed in both conventional and illegitimate attempts to lead satisfactory lives and get ahead in the society (Cloward and Ohlin 1960). These sociological theories propose that the relapse of abstaining addicts can be attributed to their returning to their old friends and haunts and to the same squalid, dismal conditions that prompted the addiction in the beginning.[7]

Most sociological theories of addiction reflect a liberal political perspective. Correspondingly, remedial efforts would focus on changing the social conditions that give rise to drug addiction, as well as other forms of social deviance, in the first place. For example, drug addiction and the relapse of ab-

7. A thorough critique of these sociological theories is provided by Clinard 1964; also see Sutter 1966.

staining addicts might be prevented if barriers to social and economic advancement, such as racism and class prejudice, could be eliminated.[8]

## Social-Psychological Theories

Social-psychological theories generally utilize either a conditioning or a learning model of human behavior. Conditioning theories argue that drug dependence is a state that results from the person's moving through a number of successive phases each of which has a different source of reinforcement (Wikler 1953, 1965, 1973). Initially, the future addict tries different drugs in different situations. Reinforcement of the drug use comes from "endogenous" sources, that is, from within the person—for example, from curiosity, boredom, or anxiety. Over time, the person may come to choose a single drug for regular use, one that satisfies some personal inclination and, perhaps, provides pleasure by reducing anxiety.

In the second phase of the process, not only does the growing tolerance to the addictive drug reduce its rewarding effects but "exogenous" sources of reinforcement are also engendered—for example, the support and encouragement of friends who are addicts. Now, if the drug is not taken, withdrawal symptoms will appear. Correspondingly, when the drug is used, withdrawal illness will be relieved dramatically. Suppression of the symptoms of withdrawal is positively rewarding and thus reinforces continued use of the drug.

From this perspective, the relapse of a person who had been abstaining is attributed to the conditioned association of withdrawal symptoms with previously neutral stimuli. For example, certain smells, such as the odor of urine, can

8. These theories provided the sociological underpinnings for many of the social programs created in the United States during the 1960s under the rubric of the War on Poverty. For two reviews of these efforts, see Marris and Rein 1967 and Moynihan 1969.

become associated with withdrawal illness because illicit street addicts often administer the drug in the relative privacy afforded by a public restroom. Thus, when an abstaining addict perceives the odor of urine, the smell may stimulate feelings of anxiety (a symptom of withdrawal). Here, drug use may be resumed in an effort to relieve the distress that is felt.

Treatment strategies suggested by conditioning theories would emphasize methods to decondition the person to both endogenous and exogenous sources of reinforcement. Drugs such as cyclazocine, which block the effects of narcotic drugs, have been advocated to be used as part of the deconditioning regimen. Blockage drugs prevent a user from experiencing the pleasurable effects of narcotics and thus eliminate an important source of reinforcement (Martin 1968).

Another kind of social-psychological theory proposes that addiction is as much a learned behavior as is any other human behavior. Typical of this approach is the work of Lindesmith (1968), who has argued that addiction occurs once the user learns to associate the symptoms of withdrawal distress with the absence of the drug. Usually, the association of withdrawal symptoms with the cessation of drug use is learned from other addicts. Once the person makes the connection and begins to use the opiate to ward off the onset of withdrawal distress, addiction occurs. If the connection is not made, then the person cannot be said to be addicted but is merely habituated.

The intentional use of opiates to prevent the occurrence of withdrawal distress has consequences beyond the personal recognition of the addiction. The individual may come to define himself as an addict and act accordingly. That is, under the adverse societal conditions that currently exist, the addict may try to make some kind of adjustment to his predicament. Because it is illegal to possess opiate drugs, and their use outside a medically approved condition is socially con-

demned, the addict is forced to act secretively and to associate with other addicts, who can help him meet the needs of
the addiction.[9]

From this perspective, the relapse of an abstaining user results from the positive attitudes toward opiates that were
learned in the early stages of the addiction. To illustrate:
Once a person who is addicted knows that opiates will relieve the stress of withdrawal and uses the drugs to relieve
that stress, he will remember this when abstinent and possibly "crave" the drugs and return to using them to relieve
feelings of anxiety or stress.

In terms of possible recovery, Lindesmith is firm in his
position that addicts, even after many years of abstinence,
cannot be said to be cured or recovered as long as they maintain positive attitudes toward opiates. In a sense, addicts can
never be cured because the knowledge that they have about
opiates and their effects can never be eradicated (Lindesmith
1968, 204). Still, Lindesmith believes that the overall lot of
illicit addicts could be improved greatly if the social stigma
associated with addiction could somehow be removed.

## Self-Initiated Recovery

Although each of the theories of opiate addiction discussed
above is different in its content, the theories are consistent
in at least one way: These theories are absolute (and pessimistic) in the belief that, without major social reform or dramatic therapeutic intervention, drug addiction is an unalterable affliction. This viewpoint parallels a similar one
held by members and supporters of Alcoholics Anonymous.
From their perspective, alcoholism, like opiate addiction, is

---

9. Lindesmith's position has been challenged on the basis of evidence
that shows that addicts do not exclusively orient their behavior to ward off
withdrawal distress but also orient themselves to achieve euphoria (see
McAuliffe and Gordon 1974).

thought to be an unalterable condition if allowed to take its "natural" course. Recovery is attained only as a result of some form of treatment.

Indeed, in spite of the fact that people may not have used an addictive substance for years following treatment, they are nevertheless still thought of as addicted. They are viewed as people who, although they may no longer be physically addicted, must still be defined as "recovered alcoholics," "ex-addicts," or "abstaining addicts," not as nonaddicts or nonalcoholics. Abstinent persons cannot drink again or use opiates on occasion; if they do, they will be certain to experience a relapse and become readdicted.

These highly deterministic perspectives are tenaciously maintained by their subscribers. As far as opiate addiction is concerned, the belief is pervasive, and it continues to receive almost unquestioned support, in spite of the existence of contrary evidence showing that addicts can and do recover, both on their own [10] and as the result of treatment (Waldorf and Biernacki 1979). More than two decades ago, Charles Winick (1962), in his "maturing out" hypothesis, suggested that addiction might be a sort of "self-limiting" phenomenon and that addicts might recover on their own (see also Maddux and Desmond 1979). Winick offered, in a somewhat vague way, a psychodynamic explanation of the reasons why some addicts quit using drugs after early adulthood. He posited that young adults become addicted as a way to cope with the problems centered in that point of the life cycle. As the problems are resolved and the young people pass into adulthood, they learn to meet the continuing challenges of life without undue stress and emotion, and thus the shrouding effects of opiate drugs are no longer desired. Consequently, they can stop their use of addictive drugs without the need

10. Evidence concerning the ways in which alcoholics recover without treatment can be found in Stall 1983 and in Tuchfeld et al. 1976, 1981.

for professional intervention. Moreover, additional evidence shows that some people, including some who were addicted earlier in their lives, can and do return to using opiates on an occasional basis in nonmedical settings without necessarily experiencing a relapse and becoming readdicted (Zinberg and Jacobson 1976).

Yet, controlled but nonaddictive patterns of opiate use, and especially the processes involved in the natural, or what might be considered the self-initiated cessation or recovery from opiate addiction, have received little, if any, substantive study or empirical analysis.

## A Theoretical Framework and a Conceptual Approach

My analysis of the processes resulting in the self-initiated recovery from opiate addiction is framed within the symbolic-interactionist tradition of sociology. Basic to this tradition is the premise that people actively construct and maintain their social worlds and act in terms of the symbolic meanings they attribute to them (Blumer 1969; Lindesmith, Strauss, and Denzin 1975; Mead 1934). Human behavior does not result from a passive process of merely reacting to some internal or external stimuli; rather, it results from an active construction and interpretation of the environment. Human beings act on the basis of how they define the various objects in their worlds, including themselves and others.[11]

Central to the symbolic-interaction perspective for understanding human behavior is the notion of "self-concept," that is, the process of making an object of one's self and the process of role taking. Ultimately, the self is acquired through interaction with "significant others." In the course of human development, the self emerges as people acquire the at-

11. Although Lindesmith generally agrees with this perspective, his classic analysis (1948), which shows the addict identity to be intractable, probably was based on the absence of contrary evidence.

titudes that significant others hold toward them. Once the self has emerged, it does not become a quiet "thing" that, now formed, is immutable. Contrary to what many psychological theories of human behavior propose, the self, from this perspective, is a process. In the course of the life cycle the self evolves and changes as people alter their associations and interpret and reinterpret the actions others take in relation to them. Human behavior, addictive behavior or otherwise, largely hinges on the conceptions that people hold of themselves and how they interpret others responding to them. Humans act according to the way in which they believe themselves to be, while they consider the possible and actual responses of others.

## Social Identities and Social Worlds

In a complex society such as our own, adults have a number of *social identities*. A social identity is the sense of place people have relative to the various groups with whom they come into contact and with whom they associate. As people move from one identity situated in a particular set of relationships to another—being a parent, student, thief, worker—a cumulative biographic image of self develops via others with whom they are commonly associated, their reference groups. These groups, real or imagined, are the ones whose opinions are valued and are used as standards to assess behavior. Correspondingly, a social identity represents the cumulative image that others hold of a particular person. In addition, identity not only encompasses the past in a biographical sense but contains a sense of the future (what people hope to be or what they fear becoming) in relation to the various social groups that they can imagine becoming part of, or of which they actually are members (Gergen 1971, 1972; Hewitt 1979).

Through the course of their lives, addicts like those of us

who pursue more "ordinary" careers, participate in a number of social worlds and correspondingly possess multiple social identities. Once acquired, some of these identities are relatively stable (e.g., parent, sibling), whereas others (e.g., student, husband, thief) are more mutable and in process. These latter kinds of identities require some maintenance and can be altered or discarded in the course of the life cycle. To varying degrees, addicts over their careers maintain membership in a variety of social worlds, each one reflecting a different social identity. Social worlds—for example, the world of medicine, the criminal world, the art world, the golf world, the world of the family, or the world of opiate addiction—are groups of people united by a network of communication and a common parlance. Members of a social world share certain representations, have a common perspective on "reality," and share particular experiences and interests (Lindesmith, Strauss, and Denzin 1975; Strauss 1978).

The interests, experiences, and perspectives on "reality" shared by illicit opiate addicts rotate around a number of interrelated occurrences: obtaining money, often illegally (called a "hustle"); purchasing the drug; obtaining the drug ("copping" or "scoring"); and using the drug ("getting off" or "fixing") (Agar 1973). From time to time, some addicts come to devote themselves almost exclusively to concerns related to their addiction and the illicit world of opiates. At least occasionally, the problems of maintaining an addiction may take precedence over other interests and participation in other social worlds. This is especially true for illicit street addicts, who may not have a ready, stable supply of the needed drug. Thus, while attempting to manage their addiction, they periodically may become immersed in the illicit world of addiction. Other addicts manage to maintain only a peripheral involvement with the world of addiction. They continue to participate in a variety of social worlds unrelated to their addiction, possibly entering the illicit opiate world only to obtain the needed drug. This variability among addicts may reflect different kinds of addicts and different kinds of involvement in the addict world (Brotman and Freedman 1968; Lewis and Glaser 1974; Stimson 1974).

The multiple identities that people, including addicts, have must be actively managed, or to use Broadhead's 1983 term, they must be "articulated." The arrangement of identities must continuously be managed in such a way as to stress some identities at certain points, in particular social worlds and situations, and at the same time to deemphasize others. This process entails the arranging of identities in relation to one another symbolically and behaviorally on the basis of interaction with oneself and others.

As I noted briefly, accompanying each identity is a perspective or point of view that is shared by other members of one's world and that, particularly in problematic situations, provides people with a general program or script for thinking and acting in relation to themselves and others. Although perspectives are social, there may not be a consensus concerning how they are defined; as a result, they can be questioned, debated, and altered intentionally.

## Social Values

A social value also is attached to each identity. Social values can and do vary with different situations and over time. People then arrange and rearrange their identities based on the relative importance they have at any time (Broadhead 1983; Hewitt 1979). For example, the social value of the addict identity may be quite high among a group of young rock musicians or among other addicts, but may carry little prestige among family members; thus, it may be symbolically and socially deemphasized in a family situation.

A rather complex social structure exists in the illicit world of addiction in which different social status is conferred depending on how well or how poorly addicts manage their habits. For example, an addict's hustle, and the style and degree of success with which it is performed, is taken by other addicts as an indication of competence and character. An addict's hustle, like a legitimate occupation in the conventional world, is used by other addicts in their evaluation of that person's social worth and in their assignment of relative status. The relationship between an addict's hustle and the social status provided in the world of addiction is important because of the profound influence it brings to bear on personal estimations of self-esteem. Thus, an addict whose primary hustle consists of various confidence games would be likely to assign a high value to the identity as a confidence man and possibly relegate a lower position to the addict identity. In contrast, a street addict who hustles mainly by "boosting" (a rather petty, unsophisticated kind of thievery) would be likely to deemphasize that identity and, perhaps, at the same time place greater value on such an identity as a trusted friend or good parent.[12]

If opiate addicts, and everyone else, have many identities, they also maintain a variety of perspectives toward themselves and others, and each perspective has a different social value. Problems may emerge for people when they try to arrange some relationship among identities in terms of their perspectives and social values. The working arrangement arrived at among problematic identities has been referred to as a *symbolic calculus,* meaning "the logic which unites multiple identities into the coherency of a person" (Broadhead 1983, 5).

In the analysis I present in this book, the calculus that people develop refers to how they articulate the addict identity, within themselves and socially, in relation to other iden-

12. For a more detailed discussion of the relationship between the social value of an identity, self-esteem, and social status in the world of heroin, see Biernacki 1979.

tities. Natural recovery refers to the process through which a new calculus or arrangement of identities and perspectives emerges and becomes relatively stabilized. This process entails a different articulation of identities in which the identity as an addict becomes deemphasized (symbolically and socially) relative to other identities existing or emerging as part of the person's overall life arrangement. Over time, the addict identity can, in some cases, become so deemphasized and distant relative to the articulation of current identities that definitions of the self as addict or junkie, along with cravings for the drug, can become almost or totally nonexistent. For others, although they may be free from opiates for years, they may still define themselves as addicts but somehow assign that identity a relatively low status and manage the craving phenomenon by using other drugs (e.g., marijuana, Valium, or alcohol). The new identities, which may, in a sense, come to fill the position of the earlier addict identity, can come about in a variety of ways, depending in part on those identities that were maintained during the addiction and the extent that the addict became locked into the world of addiction to the exclusion of participation in other worlds.

The answer to the question, How does natural recovery occur? is pursued within this conceptual framework. The answer hinges, in part, on the continued subjective and/or social existence of actual or potential identities that have not been irrevocably "spoiled" or destroyed as a direct or indirect result of the addiction (cf. Goffman 1963). The continued existence of, or possibility for, identities and their allied social worlds that are not related to the addiction provides the addict with alternative and sometimes conflicting images of self—or of what the self could be. Some analyses of addict careers argue that because of the chaotic nature of the heroin world and the related need by addicts to structure safe social networks to reduce the risk of detection and pos-

sible arrest, addicts, inevitably and uniformly, become totally immersed in the world of illicit drugs and thus spoil,
sometimes unwittingly, alternative identities (Agar 1973;
Becker 1963; Rosenbaum 1979; Schur 1965). Addicts are seen
as having few, if any, conventional associations, as having
destroyed all conventional identities that they might have
had, and as having "burned their bridges" with conventional
others in their lives. In this view, the lives of addicts become
bereft of conventional involvements, obligations, and re-
sponsibilities (Dole 1970). Increasingly, their behavior focuses on opiates—hustling, scoring, and fixing. Inevitably,
illicit addicts develop perspectives that justify unscrupulous
behavior; they come to define themselves as "dope fiends,"
"hope-to-die dope fiends," "junkie bitches," or some similar
variation.

Although the above view certainly is true, at least temporarily, in the careers of some addicts, it is not true for all addicts. For example, one perspective that corresponds with
the "dope fiend" identity justifies engaging in various criminal hustling activities to obtain money for the drug or the
drug itself. Even addicted physicians may hustle in the sense
that they violate ethical, legal, and professional codes when
they obtain and use addictive drugs. As was noted above,
however, in any social world there may be conflicting views
over what the proper perspective should be for any identity.
Thus we have disagreement among addicts concerning, for
example, the acceptability or appropriateness of hustling behavior and how to act as an addict. Some addicts are seen as
slick and smooth; others are "gutter hypes" or "snivelers."
Some addicts will steal from their families and friends;
others would never even consider such actions. Moreover,
many of the people in the study on which this book is based
defined themselves as "dope fiends" and could be considered
as having been immersed in the addict world at one time

in their lives; other respondents' claimed that they never thought pejoratively of themselves as "junkies" or "fiends," even though they were addicts. For example, a 36-year-old respondent who had been addicted for three years said, "I never considered myself a junkie. I had a bad episode for about three or four years." (032) Another respondent, addicted on and off over a twenty-three-year period and not addicted for the past twelve years, claimed that it was "funny . . . in all the time I went through it, I believed that I wasn't a hope-to-die user because I know myself. One of the other things that helped me really get away from using—I remember thinking all through my life that I wasn't a hope-to-die user." (043) Still another respondent, who had been addicted to heroin for over six years and had experienced severe withdrawal symptoms when he stopped, was asked if he ever thought of himself as a junkie? He said, "No, no. I just got high on heroin. But I didn't think of myself as a junkie." (098)[13] Contrary, then, to notions held in many quarters concerning the engulfing conditions of opiate addiction and the inevitable immersion into the illicit world of addiction, the phenomenon is not one that is experienced equally by all addicts.

### Research Methods and Criteria

*Selection Criteria*

To explore and analyze the substantive social-psychological processes that bring about a natural recovery from opiate ad-

---

13. My point here is in direct opposition to proponents of such groups as Alcoholics Anonymous, which argue that recovery can occur only after a person makes an ultimate acknowledgment of being an "alcoholic" (addict). My research shows that addicted people are able to recover because they hold out an ultimate identification for themselves of being something other than an "addict" or "junkie."

diction, the project staff set out in August 1978 and over a
two-year period managed to locate and interview 101 people
who had once been addicted to opiate drugs.[14]

The project staff recognized that people use addictive drugs
in many different ways and that the careers of addicts show
great variation. Therefore, we had to define our criteria for

14. The actual research included two groups of respondents, 101 who had
never been treated and another group of 100 who had stopped as the result
of some form of treatment. Waldorf was able to match 71 cases from each
sample (for a total of 142) on the basis of sex, age, and race. The two groups
were compared to determine whether any significant differences existed between them on certain relevant variables. The major considerations were
background characteristics that might be related to the recovery process,
motivations that the respondents reported for stopping their use of opiate
drugs, and strategies that they employed to cope with the problems they encountered while recovering. No significant differences were found between
the two groups in terms of the three broad areas of comparison.

The background characteristics included the following:

Religion

Education—those who left school before or after high school
graduation

Length of time worked and longest time worked for a single employer
before addiction

Frequency of working legitimately when addicted

Length of opiate use

Reported effects of opiates

Polydrug use

Similarly, Waldorf found no significant differences between the two
groups of respondents as to why they quit their drug use, the support and
assistance they received from others, the financial difficulties they encountered, the various coping strategies they employed, the explanations they
gave for their addiction, or the reasons they provided for their recoveries.

Although the lack of differences seems surprising, the finding is consistent with other quantitative statistical studies that have compared treated
and untreated ex-addicts (O'Donnell et al. 1976 and Robins 1973). Waldorf
attributed the absence of differences between the two groups to the possibility that the quantitative research instruments were too insensitive and suggested the use of more refined measures in future studies (Waldorf 1983).
Parts of this account are based on that study, published in the *Journal of
Drug Issues* 13, No. 2, 1983. © JDI, Inc.

addiction and recovery in ways that would be consistent with these variations. But the criteria for these definitions also had to be rigorous enough to leave little doubt that those who participated in the study had once been addicted and had recovered.

To qualify for the study, each respondent had to have been addicted for at least one year. The twelve-month total length of drug use could include more than one period of addiction, with sequences of abstinences in between.

Each respondent also had to have experienced at least five of the ten most common symptoms associated with the abrupt withdrawal from opiate drugs. The symptoms are the following:

Chills
Stomach cramps
Trouble sleeping
Nausea to the point of vomiting
Headaches
Muscle twitching
Pain in muscles
Diarrhea
Sweating and flushed skin
Running nose and eyes

Also, to qualify for the research, at the time they were screened each potential respondent had to have been free from addiction for at least the past two years. This does not mean that potential respondents were excluded if they used other drugs, or if they used opiate drugs on an occasional basis after their last addiction. A comparatively small proportion of those studied (38 people) used opiates at least once after their last physical addiction to drugs. These cases were included because they represent an important variation in the recovery process. (More will be said about these people in Chapter 4.)

Respondents were defined as having been treated for drug

addiction (i.e., not considered as having recovered on their own) if they had ever been in any formal drug treatment program for four or more days. Treatment programs included therapeutic communities, methadone maintenance, religious drug-abuse programs (e.g., Teen Challenge), psychotherapy, or regular counseling in an outpatient setting. Special parole-supervision programs that include nalline testing[15] or urinalysis were also considered to be forms of treatment, as were civil commitment programs such as those in California (California Rehabilitation Center) and New York, and the old public health hospitals in Lexington, Kentucky, and Fort Worth, Texas. Ambulatory detoxification was not included as treatment, but residential detoxification of twenty-two days or more was. Each person was screened for the above criteria before being accepted for the research and interviewed.

*Interview Schedule*

The interviews were conducted in two phases. In the first phase respondents were asked to tell what had occurred during their addiction and recovery. The interviews were guided by a schedule that included the following broad areas of inquiry:

General life situation before drug use

Life involvements, problems, extent of drug use, and self-concept before recovery

Conditions that brought about the idea to stop

Actions taken to enact the idea to stop

Role that others played in giving rise to the idea of stopping and the help that others provided to realize the idea

Problems confronted and ways in which they were handled in the process of maintaining the resolve to stop

15. Nalline testing is sometimes made a condition of parole; the effects of nalline can show whether a person has used opiates recently.

Changes undergone in self-concept, lifestyle, and ideas about the future

This phase of the interview was open-ended and was intended to have the respondents recall, in their own words, how they became addicted, what their lives were like while they were addicted, how they stopped using drugs, and the problems they had faced since they stopped. When necessary, specific probes were made for purposes of exposition and clarification. This part of the interview was tape-recorded and then transcribed into typescript for qualitative data analysis. (The entire open-ended interview guide appears in Appendix B.)

The second phase of the interview covered material similar to the first, but it was close-ended; respondents were asked to respond to specific inquiries, and their answers were recorded in precoded categories. Later, this information was used for quantitative data analysis. On the average, the interviews took about three and a half hours to complete; some interviews were done over more than a single session. In one instance, a group interview was conducted with three ex-addicts (a woman and two men) who had been interviewed separately at an earlier time. The group interview explored some of the initial ideas that had been formulated about the recovery process. Each person who participated in the study was asked to sign an informed-consent sheet, which explained the purpose of the research, listed the dangers that participation might present for the respondents, and noted the safeguards that the staff had taken to minimize any possible dangers. A twenty-dollar honorarium was provided to each person who participated in the study.

The interviews were conducted by the project staff, which was made up of four men and three women. One of the men was a Chicano and another was black; the remainder of the staff was white. Whenever possible, we tried to match the interviewer with the respondent; we were generally successful in terms of sex but less so on the basis of race. Five of the interviewers had extensive professional experience with and knowledge about addicts from past research activities. The two who did not have firsthand experience and knowledge were trained about addiction and the techniques of interviewing before they were allowed to interview respondents.

## Sampling Method

Most of the study respondents were located through referrals developed in the course of the research by using the various techniques of snowball sampling. (A detailed discussion and analysis of how the people were located for study and the overall research methodology can be found in Appendix A.) This sampling method is commonly used when the research focus is on people who, for certain moral or legal reasons, are not readily visible or easily accessible to researchers.

Locating people who qualified as untreated ex-addicts presented some challenges, but ultimately the task proved easier than we anticipated. At first, we thought that referral chains could be started through clinicians and treated ex-addicts, but we were wrong. In general, these people did not believe that addicts could recover on their own. Consequently, they were of little help in locating qualified respondents.

We started our interviewing by talking with ex-addicts whom we knew from our previous work and then asked them to refer us to other ex-addicts. At the same time, we informed our friends and colleagues about the nature of our research and asked them to refer possible respondents to the project. The success of this latter strategy, like a few other techniques, proved to be inconsistent. Sometimes it provided qualified candidates, sometimes not. The major problem in this regard was that our friends and colleagues would refer ex-addicts who had recovered on their own following unsuccessful treatment experiences.

Once we exhausted our original contacts and the chains that sprung from them, our sampling efforts turned to other areas that we thought would yield qualified respondents. Our work was not haphazard; rather, we used existing knowledge in the field of addiction to lead us to places where untreated ex-addicts might be found. For example, Robins's 1973 research on Vietnam war veterans suggested that good respondents could be located in various veteran organizations. The assumption was correct; veterans groups provided a number of good contacts. Similarly, we thought that ex-felon programs would be good sources for referrals. Our assumption was based on the current illicit status of opiate drugs and the well-known association of criminality and opiate addiction. Again, the assumption was correct; our contacts with these groups resulted in a number of fruitful referral chains. As our interviewing proceeded, we intentionally guided and shaped the referral chains, trying to get a good mix in the sample, especially in terms of sex and race.

Finally, a few chains were stimulated as the result of fortuitous contacts. In one instance, a member of the project staff attended a poetry reading where one of the reciters read a poem about his own addiction and unaided recovery. Later, the poet was interviewed; in turn, he referred three other qualified respondents to the project.

Our method of contacting and interviewing generally was consistent. We would learn of leads and would request the person who referred the potential respondents to the project to contact them and ask if they would cooperate with us. One of the staff members would then contact the prospects and screen them to determine whether they qualified for the study. If they did, an appointment for an interview was arranged.

Interviews were conducted at a place convenient for the

respondents, usually in their homes, which in some instances provided valuable firsthand information about their present lifestyles. A general policy was adopted not to accept anyone for an interview unless one of the staff members knew the person(s) who made the referral. This policy was a practical one and developed following a morning when I arrived at the office to find five current addicts waiting to be interviewed. Word had gotten around that we paid twenty dollars for each interview, so some local people thought they would try to take advantage of the opportunity. As an added precaution, we discussed all cases, especially any questionable ones, immediately after the interview to ensure that we knew the source of the referral and had not been misled. Three cases were disqualified from the study because the interviewer detected major discrepancies in the respondents' stories or because we were unable to verify the source of the referral.

## Characteristics of Study Respondents

The snowball sampling method provided a fairly diverse group of respondents. (A more detailed and complete description of the respondents is presented in Appendix C.) The addiction histories of the respondents (see Table 1) show that the length of addiction ranged from a low of one year (the minimum length to qualify) to a high of thirty years. Nearly six out of ten respondents (59 cases) reported that they were addicted for between one and four years. The next largest group (25) was addicted between five and eight years, and the remainder (17) for nine or more years. the average length of addiction for the entire group was five years and seven months (5.69 years). For nearly all respondents (94), the primary drug of addiction was heroin. The remainder (7) were addicted to opium, morphine, delaudid, or some other combination.

**Table 1.   Reported Years of Addiction[a] and Years since Addiction**

| Years | Years of Addiction, Number of Cases | Years since Addiction, Number of Cases |
|---|---|---|
| 1−2 | 28 | 14 |
| 3−4 | 31 | 29 |
| 5−6 | 19 | 23 |
| 7−8 | 6 | 16 |
| 9−10 | 5 | 5 |
| 11−12 | 2 | 6 |
| 13−14 | 1 | 2 |
| 15 or more | 9 | 6 |
| Total | 101 | 101 |
| Average | 5.69 years | 5.97 years |
| Range | 1−30 years | 2−26 years |

[a] Years addicted were calculated from first addiction to last addiction and included voluntary and involuntary periods of abstinence.

In terms of the time since they stopped using the addictive drug (again, see Table 1), the greatest number (43) of respondents said that they had not been addicted for two to four years. Twenty-three reported they were last addicted five to six years prior to their being interviewed, while the remainder (35) had not been addicted for seven or more years. The respondent who had been free of his addictive use of opiates the longest was a 47-year-old Chicano social worker, addicted for five years, who had stopped using the drug twenty-six years before he was interviewed. The average length of time that the whole group had been nonaddicted was almost six years (5.97 years).

Males made up the large majority (71) of the people interviewed. The average age of the respondents was 33.8 years on the day of the interview. Fifty-six of the respondents were between 26 and 35 years old. The youngest was 20; the oldest, 55.

Almost three-quarters (72) of the respondents were white. Chicano–Latino respondents and black respondents were nearly equal in number—14 and 12. The remainder (3) were American Indian, white Creole, and one self-identified Persian. As might be expected, given that the project was based in San Francisco, the largest number of respondents (39) were raised in California. Twenty-two grew up in northeastern states, and the next greatest number (15) came from the Midwest. Six respondents were born outside the United States. A little more than two out of five (42) respondents were raised in Catholic families. Nearly a fifth (17) came from Methodist families; 10 respondents were from Baptist backgrounds, and 6 were Jewish. A fairly large number (17) said their families did not practice a religion when they were growing up.

The educational attainment and occupations (calculated at the time of the interview) of the study participants also showed a reasonable cross-section of the general population. Whereas around one-fifth (16) never completed high school or its equivalent (GED), 9 had at least some graduate training, and a few of these respondents held graduate degrees. A quarter (26) stopped their educations when they graduated from high school, and half (50) had between one and four years of college. On the basis of current occupation, the sample included a lawyer, a few nurses, a social scientist, musicians, show-business promoters, businessmen, graduate students, seamen, construction workers, and welfare recipients.

In terms of criminal behavior, a large proportion (46) of the respondents said they had supported their addiction "mostly" through illegal activities; around one-fifth (21) reported that they supported themselves "mostly" through legitimate work, and only 3 people said they never engaged in any illegal behavior to supply their habits. Most of the participants (72) had been arrested at least once before they ended their addiction; the majority (38) of these participants were arrested between five and fifteen times. Most of the respondents (53) who reported that they had been arrested said that the arrests were for the possession or sale of illicit drugs. Nearly two-thirds (63) of the respondents said that they had been convicted of some crime; more than half (36) of these respondents reported between three and nine convictions. Overall, the respondents spent an average of more than four and one-half years (4.7 years) in jail or prison.

Determining how representative the untreated sample is of the general population of addicts or untreated ex-addicts in California is impossible because a census has never been conducted on either group. In addition, formulas created to estimate addict populations (e.g., extrapolations made from hospital emergency room admissions for drug overdoses and deaths) are notoriously unreliable.[16] Notwithstanding

16. Jerome Jaffe, former director of the President's Special Action Office in Drug Abuse Prevention, participated in the following dialogue before the U.S. Senate Subcommittee to Investigate Juvenile Delinquency on March 5, 1976:

*Senator Bayh*: Dr. DuPont, your successor, tells us there are more addicts now than there were before.

*Dr. Jaffe*: Well, since we never knew how many there were before, how do we know there are more now? I would like to see the data before one can draw that conclusion. We had great difficulty in finding a number. . . . What number are they using lately?

*Senator Bayh*: A good round number, 740,000.

*Dr. Jaffe*: If it is as precise as the number that we used to use, I have my doubts about it. . . . Senator, I can only say this: At most of the hearings where we had to present numbers, I think I drove most of the Senators to distraction by qualifications of the number. They wanted one number, and I said, now, wait a second. This number is based on a number of assumptions and here is how we got it and do not put any more weight on it, and the uncertainties that went into it. And, inevitably, I read the next day, just like you did, in all the papers that there was this one number, and it was magic, and it was fixed, and it was written on tablets of stone. I resented it just as much as you did. . . .

these problems, Table 2 shows how the study sample compares with two relevant populations. The CODAP populations (Client Oriented Data Acquisition Process) reflect the first admissions to all federally supported drug treatment programs in California that participated in the system in 1976, 1978, and 1980. The descriptive categories of the study sample were altered to make the best possible comparisons with the categories used by CODAP and the census.

Table 2 shows that the race of the study sample is similar to the California census but different from the CODAP data. There is a significantly greater number of whites in the sample than in any of the three CODAP groups. In contrast, the sexual distribution of the untreated ex-addicts compares very well with that of the CODAP admissions, but less well with that of the census. The study sample and the CODAP groups show a much larger proportion of males than exists in the 1980 California population. The study respondents also are better educated than the CODAP admissions and the California population. A greater number of those in the sample have at least twelve years of schooling than do those in the CODAP groups or those in the California census. Finally, the ages of the untreated ex-addicts are similar to those of the CODAP admissions, but somewhat older than the California population.

In terms of the occupation of the respondent's head of household, the study sample compares fairly well with the occupations reported in the 1980 California census, especially in the better-paid occupations. Table 3 shows that the study sample has fewer administrative, unskilled, and machine workers, but more clerical and skilled employees than the California census. However, if we collapse the eight occupational categories into four larger groups—higher executive–business managers, administrative personnel–clerical workers, skilled manual employees–machine operators, and unskilled–no occupation—very small differences are revealed between the sample and the census materials.

**Table 2. Race, Sex, Education, and Age of the Study Sample Compared with CODAP Admissions and the California Census**

| Category | Un-treated Sample | CODAP[a] 1976 | 1978 | 1980 | California Census[b] 1980 (18 or older) |
|---|---|---|---|---|---|
| **Race** | | | | | |
| White | 71% | 46% | 48% | 48% | 71% |
| Black | 12 | 24 | 17 | 14 | 7 |
| Chicano–Latino | 14 | 28 | 33 | 37 | 16 |
| Other | 3 | 2 | 2 | 1 | 6 |
| | | | | | |
| **Sex** | | | | | |
| Male | 70% | 72% | 68% | 68% | 49% |
| Female | 30 | 28 | 32 | 32 | 51 |
| | | | | | |
| **Education[c]** | | | | | |
| 12 years or less | 41% | 81% | 81% | 80% | 58% |
| More than 12 years | 59 | 19 | 19 | 20 | 42 |
| | | | | | |
| **Age[d]** | | | | | |
| 18–20 | 16% | 6% | 5% | 1% | 8% |
| 21–30 | 63 | 64 | 61 | 49 | 26 |
| 31 or older | 21 | 30 | 34 | 50 | 66 |
| | | | | | |
| Total $N$ = | 101 | 34,518 | 28,238 | 19,514 | 17,278,944 |

[a]CODAP (Client Oriented Data Acquisition Process) indicates number of first admissions to California drug treatment facilities. Figures are from NIDA, PHS, ADAMHA, Rockville, Md., 1976 data from Series E, No. 2 (Pub. 1977). 1978 data from Series E, No. 13 (Pub. 1979). 1980 data from Series E, No. 22 (Pub. 1981).

[b]U.S. Bureau of the Census, *1980 Census of California Population*. *Race* category from PC 80-1-B6, Table 24; *education* from PC 80-1-C6, Table 66; *Sex* from PC 80-1-B6, Table 19; *Age* from PC-1-B6, Table 18.

[c]Education of the respondents in the untreated sample calculated at the point of interviews.

[d]Age of the study respondents based on the point at which they reported to have stopped using the drug of addiction in order to make for better comparisons with the CODAP data, which is based on first treatment admissions.

**Table 3. Occupation of Respondent's Head of Household When Growing Up and California 1980 Census**

| Occupation | Untreated Sample | California Census[a] |
|---|---|---|
| Higher-level executives, proprietors, and major professionals | 18% | 18% |
| Business managers, proprietors of medium-size businesses, and lesser professionals | 8 | 5 |
| Administrators, owners, and minor professionals | 8 | 19 |
| Clerical and sales workers, technicians, and owners of small businesses | 21 | 13 |
| Skilled manual employees | 23 | 17 |
| Machine operators and semiskilled employees | 9 | 12 |
| Unskilled employees, laborers | 8 | 15 |
| No occupation (e.g., retired, students, public assistance)[b] | 3 | 1[b] |
| Refused to answer; data unavailable | 2 | — |
| Note | N = 101 | N = 11,386,075 |

[a]Census data includes only civilian labor force of people 16 years of age and older.

[b]Includes only unemployed who had no civilian work experience since 1975.

## Summing Up

The naturally recovered addicts described in this introductory chapter indicate that the conventional wisdom of "once an addict, always an addict" is a myth. Their experiences also run counter to scientific theories of opiate addiction. Most, if not all, theories about addiction are extremely pessimistic and do not even consider the possibility that at least some addicts can recover on their own, without the benefit of treatment.

The characteristics of the untreated study sample do not appear to be particularly unusual when compared with other relevant groups. Admittedly the study sample has a higher proportion of whites and is better educated than CODAP groups, but on most characteristics, the sample is very like the state's population in 1980. The differences between the sample and CODAP groups may be explained in two ways. First, whites and better-educated addicts may be more likely to turn to private clinics than to government-supported ones when they seek therapy and thus will not appear as frequently in the CODAP data. (Publicity about the apparently large number of celebrities who enter the Betty Ford Center in southern California for substance abuse reflects this point.) Second, the education of the study respondents was calculated from the time they were interviewed and not from the time of their addictions, as is done in the CODAP data. Many of the study respondents continued their education as part of their lifestyle changes after their recoveries, which may explain their comparatively higher education.

# 2

# Resolving to Stop

A life of addiction, especially under the conditions that exist in the United States at this time, is an unusually arduous one. The many problems involved in maintaining an addiction provide ample reason for people to want to stop using opiates in an addictive manner. In contrast to conventional wisdom, the instability of the heroin world and the dangers inherent in it make it almost impossible in the long run for people to maintain a strong, unwavering commitment to a life of addiction. Because this is so, there are occasions when most addicts become extremely ambivalent about their lives and decide to attempt to stop using opiates without availing themselves of a formal course of treatment.[1] (Some of the reasons for not seeking treatment when a resolution is made to give up the drug addiction are discussed in Chapter 3.)

For most addicts, the resolution to stop using opiates is rooted in a mixture of problems that grow out of addiction or the addiction in a particular context. Such problems arise when the user's addict identity affects and conflicts with the person's other identities (existing or potential) and perspectives that are unrelated to drug use. Addicts describe these conflicts as serious dilemmas that force them to a decision to continue opiate use or end it. Often, the choice about drug

1. Some of the materials in this chapter appeared in an abbreviated form in an article I co-authored with Dan Waldorf (see Waldorf and Biernacki 1981), which was published in the *Journal of Drug Issues* 11, No. 1, 1981. © JDI, Inc.

use is conceived as being one of use or abstention; occasional use is not an option. To continue to be a user entails further immersion in the world of addiction and thus shuts off the possibility of pursuing other current or potential ordinary relationships and identities. Abstention, of course, entails giving up the addiction and pursuing an alternative life course.

From time to time, most addicts come to this juncture in their lives. They consider quitting and entertain possibilities of new life involvements. For some addicts, even suicide is considered as a possible option to continuing the addiction. The intensity with which addicts come to grips with these painful choices varies greatly with the extent that their lives have been affected by the addiction. Some people manage to give up their addiction and change their lives without great emotional stress and with little conscious deliberation. For other addicts, however, the decision that results in a reorientation of their lives and perspectives to focus on more conventional pursuits is a conscious one that is both profound and excruciating.

Among the study respondents, resolutions about quitting opiates fall into three broad categories.[2] The person in the first category stops using the addictive drug but does not make a firm decision to do so. These people represent only a small number of the sample (4 to 5 percent). For addicts in the second category, ideas of quitting are developed rationally and stated explicitly. These people represent about two-thirds of the cases studied. In the third category are persons who have hit rock bottom or have experienced an existential crisis; the decision to stop emerges out of a highly dramatic, emotionally loaded life situation. These people account for one-quarter to one-third of the sample.

---

2. The numbers cited in this chapter should be taken as rough estimates; the categories were developed in the course of the research and were not explored thoroughly with every respondent.

## Quitting Without Making a Firm Decision

One of the most surprising findings of the study was that some people stop their addiction without undergoing any especially traumatic experience and without forming a conscious, explicit resolve to change. These people simply drift away from their addiction and get involved in other things; they are addicts who never developed a strong commitment to the illicit world of addiction nor came to identify themselves strongly or exclusively as addicts and accept the related perspectives. Some of them even managed to maintain interests and involvements in social worlds that were independent of those related to the addiction, and under certain conditions they simply found themselves no longer using opiates and engrossed in other life pursuits. In other instances, a change of circumstances, such as losing a job or a drug source or perhaps leaving the country where they were addicted, resulted in cessation, but without the person's consciously deciding permanently to stop using.

This gradual drifting away from the addiction and becoming involved in other life endeavors is well illustrated in an account provided by a 36-year-old respondent who had been addicted for three years. When he was asked about the last time he used heroin, he replied:

> Okay, the last time I used heroin was maybe five years ago. But the time before that had been maybe a year or so. You could just about graph it out. Having never considered myself a junkie, I never saw any reason to quit. I still don't.
>
> *Why didn't you define yourself as a junkie? You were using every day, you were living with a junkie, you were copping, and you were hustling.*
>
> I didn't want to be doing it. That was just temporary.
>
> *But you were into the life, you were into all of it?*
>
> Right.

*But somehow in your head, it wasn't there?*

Yeah. It was temporary. (032)

In the dialogue that follows, the same man describes how he gradually stopped using heroin when he became a merchant marine.

Every time I came back [to Seattle after being at sea] I'd use less and less until finally I just—

*For shorter periods of time or just smaller amounts?*

Probably both. I knew fewer and fewer junkies. You know, by this time people were dying. People were fleeing to avoid apprehension. I always had other interests. I'd been involved in trade unioning and I'd read. You do other things and you meet other people. I never considered myself to be a junkie.

*You were using—*

I had a bad episode for about three or four years.

*Did you have to get into a lot of hustling?*

Oh, yeah.

*But you kept the legal part of it going too, right?*

Yeah, but before I went to sea—going to sea really saved my ass. Up to the point I was going to sea, I was forging checks and I was about to get nailed for that. So going to sea really got me off the streets.

*How long would you be gone?*

Two or three months.

*You could have used at sea?*

Yeah, but how much stuff are you going to take to sea with you? I never took any. Some guys do. I used some.

*But it wasn't like you were going to sea to cop when—*

No, I was going to work. (032)

This man had maintained an interest in politics and social reform while he was addicted and gradually became increasingly involved in labor organizing; eventually, he became a union steward. Although he claimed that he never made a conscious decision to stop using heroin, at the time of the interview he had not been addicted for nine years.

Another man, who had used heroin over a span of six years, never consciously resolved to quit but gradually stopped using and simply drifted away from the addict world after he lost a job. He was working on a cotton farm in California and taking home around $300 a week in wages, most of which went to purchase heroin. He explained:

> Eventually, I got hooked—like where if the drug's out, I couldn't work, I had to go find some—and I lost my job. The only thing I could do was move in with my parents again, which was in Santa Cruz. Fortunately, I didn't know anyone in Santa Cruz and I didn't have a car or any money. So I couldn't go back to Bakersfield to score. I lived there for about a year, and during that year I fixed a couple of times. And then after a couple of years somehow you become rational and you look at heroin as a normal person. It's not the only thing in your life. It's not the most important thing. Not the only important thing. (100)

In still other instances, people quit their drug use without actually deciding to do so as the result of situational changes. It is a fact that some people become addicted, and remain addicted, less as a result of their own doing than as a result of the actions of others. Let me illustrate this: A person may be in a dependent relationship with another person who supplies the drug and encourages its use. Typically, the dependent person is relatively young and relies on the other not only to supply the drug but also to provide companionship, direction, and some semblance of security. Cessation of drug use in such instances commonly occurs when the dominant person is removed from the relationship by, for example, illness, imprisonment, or death.

One 23-year-old woman became addicted in London when she was 17 years old. She was a citizen of the United States, and her parents had sent her to live in a convent in Ireland. Feeling abandoned and lonely, she ran away from the convent and eventually ended up living with an addicted man, who introduced her to opiates. She became addicted, and he supplied their drug needs by burglarizing pharmacies. At one point he was arrested, and she stopped using for six months while he was in jail. When he was released, they reunited and resumed their old pattern of pharmacy burglaries and drug use. Eventually they were both arrested, and she was confined in prison before being deported to the United States. In the following dialogue she explains how she felt at that time:

> *Were you thinking of giving up drugs during that period?*
>
> I knew that was it.
>
> *You knew that was it? In other words, your drug use was tied to him. When he went away and you left England, that was it. No more opiates after that?*
>
> Yes, it was really strange. (096)

Later in the interview, she noted that she "didn't feel she was really herself" when she was addicted. She observed:

> Well, it was just like a thing that overcomes you. Like . . . overtakes your personality. Once in a blue moon your real self peeks out, "Oh my God, what is this?" It goes, "Never mind, I don't want this." Then the monster thing takes over again.
>
> *You felt incongruous in that world?*
>
> It's like being a zombie for three years. There was no real love there or any care or anything to do. It was real strange.

*So it really wasn't you?*

No.

*You just sort of fell into an activity—a lifestyle that was out of keeping with you, but you went along with it?*

Yeah. (096)

When the relationship with her addicted boy friend was severed, she stopped using drugs. She never made a resolve to quit, yet, at the time of the interview, she had not been addicted for three years.

Still other people can stop using opiates without a strong, conscious resolve to do so because they never develop an image of themselves as addicts. They maintain other interests and perspectives and never come to believe that developing a physical addiction to opiates is something they cannot readily overcome. One 40-year-old man became physically addicted to opium while traveling in Turkey, Iran, and Afghanistan during the late 1960s. He smoked and swallowed opium on a daily basis for three years. He did not think of himself as a strong-willed person, but he had no trouble giving up his opiate use when he left Iran for Europe following an arrest for possession of hashish. Asked whether he simply stopped using when he felt his drug habit was getting out of hand, he replied:

No, I usually continued it for a while longer and then I would stop. I wish I could say I don't continue stuff. No, I wouldn't say that I was a real strong-willed person. I'm not like that. (099)

At another point in the interview he made the following observation about the occasional breaks he took from using opium:

I never looked on it as a particularly big thing I was about to do. It didn't compare, for example, to stopping from smoking cigarettes. (099)

When he was asked how he came to stop using opium, he simply said, "Well, I left the East." (099) The interviewer was rather surprised by his answer and asked, "You simply left the East, and that was it?" He responded:

> No, not at all, because you can get it [opium] in the next country. They had opium dens there if I wanted to. I smoked marijuana continuously for about thirteen or fourteen years and I never even thought of it [opium] during the time. (099)

The situational change that this man underwent resulted in his giving up the opium addiction. And he changed his behavior without experiencing any apparent serious difficulties.

When we listen to responses like these, we seriously question the widely held assumption that the physically addictive properties of opiates are so powerful that an addiction to them cannot be broken without the person's experiencing great emotional and psychological trauma (Coleman 1978). The message in these responses seems to be that some people become physically addicted but do not come to believe that they cannot do without the drug. Should their situations change so that they are temporarily separated from a source for the drug, they may gradually use less and less until they discover, sometimes only in retrospect, that they no longer are addicted. In a sense, they are able to walk away from their drug use without ever resolving to do so.

## Explicit, Rational Decisions to Stop

Many addicts come to a point in their lives where they rationally and explicitly decide to stop using opiates. Often this point occurs after a cumulation of negative experiences coupled with some particularly significant and disturbing personal event. These experiences usually are expressed in terms of serious conflicts between continued drug use and other desires. For example, addicts fear what might lie ahead should they continue using, or they tire of dealing with the problems of addiction (see Jorquez 1983), or they experience conflicts between their addiction and other identities and interests they have maintained. The significant personal experiences that may result in actual attempts to stop using opiates, as one would expect, vary greatly from one individual to another. Some of these events are quite dramatic—the loss of a loved one, for example—while others, in comparison, seem to the outsider rather mundane or even trivial, such as the inadvertent purchase of poor-quality heroin.[3] The events are similar, however, in that they serve to shatter addicts' complacent attitudes about their addiction and awaken perspectives rooted in identities that are not related to the use of opiates.

One man in the study became addicted while serving as a corpsman with the marines in the Vietnam war. He was using his own supply of morphine ampules, and his addiction seemed to be functional in that the effects of the drug helped mask some of the psychological and emotional pain he was experiencing about the war. He described his drug use as follows:

> I had a feeling of somewhat peacefulness, that I was detached somewhat from the emotional part of seeing what I was seeing, and I kept using. (002)

He felt guilty; he was very uncomfortable with the part he played in the war, but he also felt great compassion for his comrades and their plight. When he was seriously wounded and returned to the United States, he had a large supply of morphine he had secreted in his medical dressings. At the time, opposition to the war was at its peak, and he participated in an antiwar march staged in San Francisco with

---

3. Knupfer (1972) also reported finding what seemed to be rather undramatic experiences preceding the recovery of alcoholics. She referred to these events as "strangely trivial reasons."

some active-duty soldiers. He described the conflicts he felt at the time and how they influenced his decision to stop using:

> I participated in that march and got somewhat turned off by it because of people just saying, "Vietnam, the soldiers, killers." I knew we were killers, but I also knew it wasn't all of our responsibility. I got angry. I remember, if they were right, then my buddies died for nothing. Then the Vietnamese died for nothing. And I remember feeling that anger, and it was very hard for me to feel anything when I was using—any emotion. That anger just seemed to get on top of the need for the drug, so I threw them [the syrettes] away. (002)

Soon after this episode, he went to the eastern city where he had grown up, and with the help of some friends he withdrew from the morphine. Later, he returned to the San Francisco Bay area and turned his anger to social and political action to benefit other veterans.

A 45-year-old man who had been addicted for six years described the conflicts he felt and his decision to stop using as follows:

> The one thing I did know was that I didn't want to be known as a tramp and I didn't want to feel like a nobody, a nothing. I was a very proud person, so I had to do something about those drugs. Either it was going to control me, or control my life, or I was going to stop using. My goals were the good old U.S. American dream that everybody has. (052)

Often, the subjective conflicts of addicts are coupled with deep fears of what might happen to them should they continue using. Personal observations and knowledge of what has been the fate of other addicts can heighten their fears that the addiction will completely ruin other actual or po-

tential aspects of their lives, and this possibility can be sufficient for them to decide to change.

The considered nature of the kind of situation that can
lead to a resolve to stop using opiates was well described by a
man who had used heroin for more than a decade. During
the period of his addiction, he was employed as a social
worker. He did not engage in many criminal actions. He was
feeling depressed because of the serious financial problems
that he was facing as a result of his addiction. He recalled
how he decided to quit:

> So I knew . . . the only way I was going to be able to man-
> age it was to start dealing, and I didn't want to take the
> chance on dealing, of getting busted. And second of all, to
> deal I'd have to be available all the time at strange hours. I
> couldn't have people call me up at work to score. So, I just
> like decided that was not going to be possible and that it
> was going to require an enormous change in my whole life
> to survive in terms of dope. So I sat down and thought to
> myself: "Would I be willing to trade the rest of my life for
> dope?" And the answer was, "Yes, I would if I could in-
> sure myself of a regular, steady supply." But in that sort of
> game you usually get busted sooner or later. So, I say, I en-
> visioned the future as trading my life for dope and then
> winding up, also, out of dope. And I could see it wasn't
> going to work. It finally became clear that this was the
> end. I was going to have to make a big change, of my whole
> life. And I wasn't willing to make that change because I
> didn't think it would work. So that's why it was kind of a
> rational decision. (071)

Another respondent, a 32-year-old woman who was addicted
to heroin for three years, made a similar decision to stop
when she finally faced the fact that the costs of her habit had
grown far beyond what she could afford on the salary she was
making. She recounted how she had seen her life taking a
change for the worse:

I was real scared, real frightened, real terrified . . . of what would happen to me. I felt like I was at a point where either I had to clean up or become a dealer or prostitute, live on Main Street in downtown L.A.

*In other words, things were going to change for you, change for the worse?*

Yeah, I didn't think how they could possibly do anything but that. (077)

Some addicts, then, resolve to change their lives and stop using opiates when the option of continuing to use drugs entails consequences that are simply far too undesirable in terms of the view they have of themselves and their future lives. At this point they rationally weigh each possibility and decide that they have much more to gain by breaking the addiction than by continuing it.

For still other addicts, the motivation or idea to stop using drugs results from the general vicissitudes of a life of addiction. In many ways, the addicts' situation is similar to that of the "burnout" phenomenon experienced by nonaddicts who work in occupations that are emotionally charged and stressful and that require them to meet a continuous flow of problems with professional detachment and personal enthusiasm. After many years, these people find that they cannot do it anymore; they may continue to meet their obligations, but do so spiritlessly, with little or no enthusiasm. Addicts, especially illicit street addicts, also burn out in a sense. They tire of dealing with the myriad problems involved in managing their addiction. This situation is most typical of people who have been addicted for comparatively longer periods of time. Often, they express their "burnout" in terms of being tired—they are tired of "the life," the "changes," of other junkies, and of going to jail.

The problems that addicts encounter result from the pressures that society places on them. The illegality of opiates means reduced drug supplies and fluctuating quality, high prices, police surveillance and arrest, and general stigmatization. Some addicts eventually tire of the cycles of being high one day and sick the next.[4] There is a cumulative effect that comes from the constant threat of arrest, the exploitive and self-centered behavior of other addicts, and the spending of so much time in jail. For many addicts, these are chronic problems; they weary of dealing with them, particularly as they grow older.

The general chaotic state of the addict condition often results in addicts' thinking about altering their lives and stopping their use of opiates, and should this be coupled with a significant negative personal experience, it can result in the addict's resolving to change. For some addicts, the personal experiences that stimulate the resolve seem to be rather trivial events—for example, purchasing poor-quality heroin ("bunk") and not being able to get high. Yet, to the addict these events may not be trivial at all; added to the other problems the addict must deal with, they are perceived as being "the last straw." Let me illustrate this point: Street addicts who are not large dealers must work very hard to satisfy their addiction. Most of them spend a great deal of time and energy hustling to obtain money for the drug, eluding the police, avoiding being robbed by other addicts, and attempting to ensure that they purchase good-quality drugs. When withdrawal symptoms start to appear, they look forward with great anticipation to experiencing the relief and euphoria the drug can provide. If the drug turns out to be of such poor quality that it yields only minimal, if any, satisfaction, the addicts' consequent feelings of extreme disappoint-

4. Ironically, the well-known problems and dangers involved in being an illicit addict are not enough to dissuade many young people from experimenting with opiate drugs. In fact, the numerous hazards associated with addiction serve to entice some youth to use opiates; the risks represent a challenge, and by using drugs they can enhance their status and reputations in the eyes of their friends (see Feldman 1973; Sutter 1966).

ment are understandable. Their anger may be directed at others in their world, but it is directed as well at themselves, and this may be enough to shake their perspective and allow for the serious consideration of alternatives to their plight.

That an apparently trivial event can disturb an addict's equilibrium and trigger a resolve to quit using opiates can be seen in the account provided by a 29-year-old man. He had been addicted to heroin for four years and even avoided induction into the army during the Vietnam war because of his addiction. He borrowed and stole money from his family, sold highly adulterated heroin, burglarized a pharmacy, was robbed by other addicts, broke up with his first wife, and got his second wife addicted before he decided to stop. Yet the event that corresponded with his final resolve to quit seems almost petty compared with what he had gone through. As he recalled it:

> Another real motivating factor was I copped a bunch of dope in San Diego and was going to Oregon to sell it. It was four or five times as [expensive] up there. While I was up there, she [his wife] ran out of dope and went to the ghetto to cop and my connection just freaked. He told her to get the fuck out of there and never come back. It was just insane for a white lady to be walking down there. That scared the hell out of me. When I got back and she told me the story, I said, "That's it, we're getting out of here!" (036)

The couple moved in with his parents, who were not aware of the young people's addictions. The husband told his parents that they had the flu. After about six weeks with his parents, the couple moved into a place of their own. He started drinking heavily; their relationship strained and finally broke. More than a year later, he began to control his drinking, was reunited with his wife and daughter, and has not used any opiates since.

The growing weariness that many addicts develop as a result of having to deal with the myriad problems posed by their addiction can readily be seen in an account provided by a 55-year-old former addict. This man had been addicted for thirty years and had been imprisoned many times. Asked what had brought him to his decision to stop, he replied:

> Well, the way my life had taken a change. I wasn't getting anywhere. I didn't want to [steal]. I didn't want to continue. I just had it. I was always waiting, you know, waiting to steal something or waiting to score. [And] stuff [heroin] wasn't like it used to be. I was averaging six [fixes] a day. It was taking all my [pay] checks.

> *You were getting tired. What did you do about it?*

> Well, what did I do about it, I quit. I just got tired of it. I said, "Well, I have no money. Ain't got no clothes or nothing. This is going to be the last one." I got down and then busted up the outfit. I was just tired. Tired of doing what I had to do to stay loaded, and I wasn't staying loaded. (038)

Another man in the study had been addicted for twelve years. He had been a heroin dealer, a burglar, and a robber. He had done time in county jails and prisons in Oklahoma and California. His second marriage was on the verge of breaking up when he came to the point of deciding to quit. He described the point quite simply when he said that he "was tired of being sick and tired." (076)

## Hitting Rock Bottom and Existential Crises

As I have shown, the findings of this study only partly support earlier studies concerning how *treated* ex-addicts come to a point where they decide to quit (Brill 1972; Coleman 1978). Other researchers generally agree that certain psychological states of "rock bottom" or "existential crisis" are posited as necessary preconditions to successful recovery, but the testimony of this study's respondents indicates that such crises are not essential; some persons experienced them, and others did not.

The two phenomena—hitting rock bottom and experiencing an existential crisis—have not been clearly distinguished in the literature. *Rock bottom* is defined here as a subjective state; it is the point at which people reach the nadir of their lives and decide, with some emotion, that they must change. For example, they may experience deep humiliation as a result of being robbed or jailed, or they may feel socially rejected when they learn that significant others are now aware of their addiction. Drug use and the addict lifestyle may become intolerable, and a decision to change is made.

*Existential crisis* can be distinguished from the rock-bottom phenomenon by the fact that an existential crisis is a more profound emotional and psychological state. Addicts in the midst of an existential crisis come to question their whole life pattern and, within that pattern, their core identities as drug addicts. Most commonly, the experience is felt in terms of profound mortification, as a symbolic death of the self (see Berger and Luckmann 1966; Burke 1954). Because some addicts engage in contemptible behavior when trying to support their habit, they may feel scorned by others; they feel guilty and degraded. Recognizing the reasons for feeling as they do, they may try to salvage some vestige of their sense of self-worth by considering various social options to their quandary, but because of what they have done and what they believe others think about them, they may conclude that they have nowhere to turn. Unable to reclaim some positive sense of worth, they may turn to thoughts of suicide, or actual suicide attempts, as the only way to relieve their suffering.

Hitting rock bottom and experiencing an existential crisis are the conditions most commonly associated with the emergence of thoughts about stopping their drug use among addicts who have become the most immersed in the illicit world of addiction, to the exclusion of participation in other, more conventional worlds. The depth of the immersion is not merely related to the length of the addiction; it has more to do with the behavior of those addicted. Regardless of the length of time of the addiction, some addicts behave in such untoward ways as virtually to destroy any conventional relationships and identities they may have had; others are very circumspect in their behavior and thereby preserve at least some existing or potential involvements and identities that are unrelated to the addiction.

The emotional depth of the rock-bottom crisis was well described by a 26-year-old woman who had been addicted for three years before she stopped using. Asked what brought her to the point of stopping, she explained:

> I felt bad about it. I felt bad about myself. That time I was in jail I just—after I kicked, you just start doing all this thinking—wow! I just really felt bad about myself. I didn't like all the shit I was doing to other people and to myself. Then it's a very risky life. If you're hurting and you don't feel like going out and ripping off. Or you don't have a car . . . we didn't have a car. Then you have to worry about all that too, getting killed or OD'ing. I thought I was worth more or should do more. I felt terrible about myself. I was sick. My face was all messed up, broken out. I wanted to get out of it. (013)

Another respondent, a 37-year-old woman who had been addicted for almost six years and at the time of the interview had not been addicted for nearly fourteen years, also reached a rock-bottom point just before quitting. Her description of the severe humiliation and degradation she felt at the time, which is particularly compelling but not at all an unusual reaction among both male and female ex-addicts, follows:

> I did a couple of hustling scenes. I remember one that just really nauseates me. It makes me want to puke. You know, a really old man who couldn't get an erection, you know all the numbers you've got to go through. Some of the sexual things were bad. That is really low, having to do that kind of thing. It's one thing to lie down and get fucked, but it's another thing for some shitting old creep that couldn't do shit anyhow—oh, God! That was bad news! I ripped off some people. It bothers me that I ripped off. I've ripped off some people that were friends. That bothers me. I have laid in my own urine—stuff like that. That's all part of the ultimate degradation. (011)

Although people who undergo rock-bottom crisis just before stopping their drug use may feel extremely bad about themselves and what they have done, they usually do not report having had suicidal thoughts or actions at the time. The thought of taking one's own life as an alternative to continuing the addiction is a major factor that distinguishes the rock-bottom phenomenon from the existential crisis. The existential crisis is felt as a sense of mortification where the most profound kind of self-questioning occurs and where the individual feels that he has nowhere to turn to salvage a sense of well-being or self-worth. Suicide is considered to be a better alternative than remaining in such an undesirable social and psychological state.

Sixteen of the people who participated in our research study, or about one-sixth of the respondents, had undergone an existential crisis before stopping the use of opiates and changing their lives. One rather well educated respondent, who had used heroin for over twenty years, reported how he went through such a crisis when he was 33 years old.

I was really serious. I didn't want to die of a drug overdose necessarily because that was really tacky—you die suffocating. That's not what I had in mind. So I bought a .357 [a large-caliber handgun] and I thought, "I'll blow my brains out." A drug addict does not have a life. So I sit down on the weekend and I have a very, very reflective weekend. I say to myself, "I'm thirty-three years old. I'd gone through careers that would have made anybody happy half loaded." But, I said to myself, "I'm going through more money than most ever had a chance to. I don't have a pot to piss in; I don't have anything. I don't have any friends who aren't dealers or users; my entire social life is spent copping drugs or watching a late night movie. I don't go fishing; I don't play ball; I don't have a life." I couldn't get a vein up anymore. I had tracks [marks on the skin from needle injections] up like roads. You reach the point where you can't get high anymore. So I said to myself, "I'm either going to stop doing it and try to make a life for myself at thirty-three. It's probably too late. I've blown too much. I have no relatives . . . I can talk to. I don't have a home. I don't own anything. I've burned anyone I've been involved with. I'm ashamed of what I've done on a human basis. People I know are just as likely to steal my TV as kill me. Is this a life? I'm either going to blow myself away or clean it up." (089)

Another man, addicted to heroin and morphine for five years, came to a similar point in his life. Asked whether he had thoughts of death or suicide just prior to his stopping, he recalled:

Yes, very strongly, just before the money ran out, to the point where I had a .38 [handgun] to my head but I couldn't pull the trigger. I put it right here [pointing to his temple], and I loaded up and I'd take the bullet out and I'd pull the trigger. You know, put the bullet back in, couldn't do it. I

finally made up my mind to do it. What's the first thing I
do? I cover the whole floor with a plastic bag so I don't ruin
the carpet for the landlord! You know, now I laugh about it.
[But] there was absolutely no hope. I was scared to death.
(028)

Instead of committing suicide, with great trepidation this
man opted to change his life and to pursue a life without
narcotics.


**Summing Up**

Addicts seem to be rather complacent when things are going
well. When their lives hold some personal satisfaction and
provide them with a sense of self-worth, they do not question their condition or make commitments to change. For
most addicts, particularly those who are almost totally immersed in the world of addiction, some significant (to them)
experience has to jolt them into a new perspective on reality
and result in their questioning themselves and their lives as
addicts. Those addicts who maintain involvements in other
social worlds, or those who become addicted as a result of
"just going along," may not explicitly or firmly resolve to
stop using drugs. For addicts such as these, the cessation of
drug use often has the quality of "just happening."

When thoughts of quitting drugs are rooted in major life
crises, addicts experience deep fears that continued drug use
will prove detrimental to their well-being, perhaps their very
existence. The various problematic situations that stimulate
thoughts of stopping the use of opiates and changing one's
life, especially if they result in a strong, conscious resolve to
do so, are particularly important in understanding the processes through which a rational recovery from opiate addiction can occur. These situations seem to have a common
effect in that they bring about a fundamental reorientation

of the person's frame of reference and perspective. Interests and actions that once could be considered necessary, or at least could be justified, or perhaps were even thought of as appropriate when the person was addicted—for example, stealing to support the addiction—now are seen as quite the opposite, as unjustifiable and undesirable. This shift represents at least a partial turning away from what one was or might become, and commences a search for other ways to fulfill one's life.

In certain instances, the resolve to change may be given added impetus because the problems that gave rise to thoughts of change are situated in the world of addiction and may make it difficult, if not impossible, to continue safely an illicit life of addiction. For example, out of a sense of desperation an addict may identify a dealer to the authorities; as a result, the addict has become known as a police informant. In this situation, it could be extremely dangerous for the informant to continue a life of addiction. The danger thus adds force to the resolution to change.

The change of perspective that occurs at problematic points or times of crisis in the lives of many addicts was described in a variety of ways by the people in our study. For some addicts, the reorientation seemed to take place rapidly, almost overnight; for others, the change was more gradual, developing over days or even months. One person who described how his perspective changed obtained a master's degree in psychology after recovering from his addiction. He was addicted to heroin for more than three years and was last addicted eight years before the interview. He recalled that his becoming addicted was like fulfilling a childhood dream:

> . . . because it was fulfilling a childhood desire, because most people that I knew and idolized as a kid were hypes [addicts]. They were people that were taking care of business [doing what is necessary to manage the addiction]. . . .

So, even though I was somewhat aware of the politics, it didn't go any further than just conversation, talking . . . then after a while I had to get further and further back. I realized I had to come out of this, because it was leading up into down, and it was like hell. I saw what it was doing to their [older addicts] bodies. Losing their teeth. A lot of them didn't have any teeth. I saw guys, I mean we would get loaded and talk about politics, talk about religion, we'd talk about school systems, and these people weren't dummies! Some of them were artists. They used to draw, write poetry, but they . . . it wasn't functional. They couldn't use it in terms of helping themselves or the community or anything. It wasn't anything, it wasn't positive in the community. So I wanted to be more. I wanted to do more. (045)

Another man, who had been addicted to opium for five years in Iran, described how he used to resent people who were not addicted because of the freedom they exercised without having to be concerned about drugs. His perception of his dealer started to change when he was deciding to stop using; he began to perceive his dealer in a different and negative way.

I did feel a little uncomfortable with people who were not addicts at certain points in my life because they could do a lot of things I couldn't. They were free, and I always considered myself a slave, and it sort of gave me this feeling of jealousy. But it's true, I did want to feel free and I still did want to use. But I couldn't do both at the same time. And my relationship, then it turned into a business relationship. He was still my friend, but I was buying from him, you see. And, yes I did begin to feel different about him because I felt one up on him. He was . . . addicted for twenty years. He was in a situation, his walking was different. His speech was slurred. I didn't want to be like him. A lot of times I said, "God, I don't want to be like him." You know, shaky hands, but you see it's very hard to give priorities to what you want in life. (081)

With thoughts of quitting and, possibly, a resolve to do so, once-positive points of reference become negative ones in assessing interests and life involvements. Alternatives to the life of addiction are actively considered. The problem for recovering addicts at this point is to decide what to do with their lives as an alternative to the addiction and how to deal with the uncertainty that they can function, or even live, without opiates.

# 3

# Breaking Away from Addiction

In the last chapter I showed that under present societal conditions, the lives of illicit opiate addicts can be exceedingly difficult. A life of addiction is pursued in a confounding maze; there are potential and actual dangers at every turn. The endless series of problems that addicts confront and the failures they endure provide them with ample reasons to want to stop using drugs.

This chapter focuses on the problems that addicts face when they attempt to shift the direction of their lives dramatically and stop using addictive drugs. It explains the steps involved in the process of becoming abstinent, examines the conditions that shape the various pathways to quitting, and describes the strategies that addicts use to break away from the world of addiction.

## Restraints on Becoming Abstinent

As any cigarette smoker knows, resolving to end the habit may not result in taking action that *will* end it. Similarly, a resolution to stop using opiates does not necessarily indicate that the corresponding action will ensue. Over the course of their addiction, addicts frequently make and break the resolutions they have made to themselves and others. Even when resolutions to stop using are coupled with a disturbing personal experience that may prompt actual attempts to abstain, the effort may not succeed. Addicts who experience the cycles of abstinence and relapse, and who witness others attempting to abstain but failing, provide substance for the belief that "once an addict, always an addict" (see Ray 1961). According to this belief, addicts simply cannot sustain voluntary attempts at abstinence; invariably they will return to using the addictive drug.

This disparaging comment about the addict world, sometimes uttered with expressions like having an "addictive personality" or being "a hope-to-die dope fiend," finds support not only among addicts but also among segments of the medical and professional communities.

One woman in the study recalled what happened when a physician who was treating her for pneumonia discovered that she was addicted to opiates.

> He noticed my tracks, and he said, "Wait a minute, I'll be right back." And I heard him go into the next room, and he was talking to another doctor, and I overheard him. He said, "That's another damn junkie in there. Once you're a junkie, you're always a fucking junkie." Exact words he said. I said, "Wow." And it just made me so mad. (078)

Although such pessimistic attitudes and put-downs probably affect the lives of addicts in a distressing variety of ways, one thing is sure: They certainly work to inhibit the formation of a strong resolve to stop using and to undermine a resolve once it is formed. The addict who accepts the belief that addicts can never recover from their addiction may halfheartedly attempt to stop using, but will abandon the attempt in the face of the first adversity. Who wouldn't?

### The Absence of Recovery Models[1]

Addicts who are setting out to end an opiate addiction on their own face an uncertain future. There is little, if any, sub-

1. This section about the absence of ex-addict role models grew out of discussions with Eddie Washington, a member of the project staff.

cultural folklore to give them insight into how they might go about ending their addiction. In fact, they may feel that they are treading a path where no one has gone before. The reason for the dearth of recovery models for addicts who are trying to stop using is that people who become and remain abstinent without treatment generally cease to associate with those who remain addicted. Indeed, ending such associations, as I show later in the chapter, is in most instances a necessary condition for becoming abstinent, especially during the first year or so.

During the course of our research, we discovered that very few referrals to untreated ex-addicts were being made by ex-addicts who received treatment. Most treated ex-addicts were highly skeptical of the possibility that addicts could recover without treatment. This skepticism partly stems from the fact that naturally recovered ex-addicts usually do not continue to associate with addicts—they isolate themselves from the world of addicts. The nonbelief also may be rooted in the treated ex-addicts' own past experiences of repeated relapses following voluntary attempts at abstinence and their perception that their current drug-free state is the result of the success of the drug treatment.[2] Thus, few, if any, stories circulate in the addict world about people who have succeeded in their voluntary efforts to stop further opiate use. And those addicts who try to quit, but fail, commonly return to the addict world and serve to reinforce existing beliefs in the futility of attempting to quit without undergoing a formal course of treatment.

## The Uncertain Quality of Resolutions

Understandably, addicts who come to the point where they resolve to stop using drugs are doubtful about whether they

2. For a more thorough discussion of this point, see the methodology section in Appendix A.

can abstain successfully and permanently. Many of the respondents in our study remembered their initial resolutions to stop using drugs as being weak or fragile, in terms that suggested they were by no means certain that they would actually be able to enact and maintain the decision. During a group interview (described in the first chapter) with three study participants who had been interviewed separately at an earlier time, one of the men described the vulnerable nature of his initial resolve to stop using:

> . . . for me the resolve was fragile, and I needed to protect that. I mean, I wanted, maybe not consciously . . . I felt uncomfortable about my use and finally, when I did decide, I knew what an uphill battle it would be to really go ahead and stay clean. I felt like I had to muster all of the resources I had to stay clean. I felt I would easily succumb to a close friend of mine who I like, I cared to spend time with, who wanted to do me a favor. Who wanted to do a kind thing for me by turning me on. It was difficult for me to really say, "No, I want to be different than you." It requires also a denial of where the other person is coming from. Those kinds of issues—to really deal with them in a clear, straightforward manner was not something I could really do. So the resolve that I have, I had to protect. (Group interview)

The uncertainty felt by addicts who are contemplating a radical change in the overall arrangement of their lives is probably quite similar to the experiences of nonaddicts who are considering or undergoing an extreme and abrupt life alteration. Such feelings of uncertainty and trepidation are common, for example, when a partner in a long-standing marriage suddenly decides to leave it, or when a person decides after many years to change an occupation. The problem for addicts is intensified, however, because now they must deal with such feelings as anxiety, something that they may not have done for years because any anxiety that may have been felt was masked by the effects of opiates. In all likelihood the strength of the uncertainty and anxiety is greatest among those addicts who have come to be most caught up in the world of addiction and who have participated in other, more conventional social worlds infrequently. The problems revolve around such basic issues as what to do with themselves and their lives. What will take the place of the addict lifestyle? They harbor serious doubts about whether they can establish and maintain relationships with "ordinary" people, that is, those who are not addicted. Of course, at the back of their minds is the uncertainty they feel about whether they can change their lives and remain free of opiates at the same time.

Addicts who have managed to maintain good relationships with people who are not involved in the world of addiction generally have an easier time moving through this period and realizing their desire to change their lives. They can find support among those relationships that have not been destroyed and can emphasize the identities situated in them. Other addicts have a much more difficult time implementing their resolutions because of the absence of perceived alternatives to their present situation. They may think that they have "burned their bridges" and that they cannot reinstitute past relationships with family or friends. They also may think that they are unemployable, and they may be right in the assumption. Many of these addicts have criminal records, poor employment histories, or a lack of salable skills. And after many years of addiction, they may think that they do not know how to act when looking for a job or that they do not have appropriate clothing to wear to a job interview. All in all, they have many and often justifiable fears that they will not be able to get along with people in the conventional world.

The precarious feelings that addicts had when they were

at the point of deciding to stop were well described by one man. As he was advising other addicts about what to do if they wished to stop their drug use and change their lives, he admonished:

> I've worked very hard on becoming clean and staying clean. I would suggest that if there are any junkies out there that are thinking about quitting, do it. Even if you think, "What the hell am I going to do after I quit?" I thought that too, and I didn't know. I had a couple of ideas, but I didn't know. Don't worry about that, just go and take the first step. Let whatever happens, happen. (017)

Another man, who had been addicted to heroin for two and one-half years, recalled the uncertainty he felt at the time he resolved to stop using drugs:

> I had taken every drug there was. I'd been in all the social situations, sexual situations, traveled an awful lot, and I really didn't see what the hell I was going to do. I was really kind of concerned with that. (085)

At times, the problems and concerns of maintaining an addiction can be so intense that addicts can become almost completely isolated from people who are not addicted and can find themselves living outside contemporary societal concerns. The problems that can come about as a result of such isolation were dramatically described by one respondent. He recalled that shortly after he quit using, he boarded an airplane while he was carrying a loaded gun. He was completely unaware that airports had increased electronic surveillance and security in response to the rash of hijackings that were taking place. Obviously he had not read a newspaper or watched a TV news broadcast in a long time. Fortunately for him, the weapon went undetected, and he escaped almost certain arrest.

Another respondent, an addict for four years, described the social dilemma that addicts face when they decide to stop using, especially the absence of support from conventional others. He began by reflecting about the self-examinations he went through while he was in jail.

You know, it's easy to analyze yourself and all your mistakes when you are in jail because you don't have anything else to do but that, and you can see where you went wrong. You figure out how you're going to clean up that next time where you won't do that again. But when you come out and you have no one to go to and nothing to go to, you don't have the support that you need. Like a dope fiend comes out and goes directly to a group of dope fiends because these people are going to say, "Hey, man, how are you doing? Welcome back! You got any money, brother? Come on, I know who's got the best dope in town." The guy knows he's got a shot coming. You know, he's going to be glad to see you. These are the people that accept you. I am a dope fiend and I have problems thinking that all the guys down at the gym are going to accept me right away to play basketball, are going to accept me right away because I ain't hanging out with them at all. So I would be uncomfortable in going with them. But if I go with the dope fiends, I ain't going to be uncomfortable. But if you go to another group of people and you start talking a certain way and acting a certain way, then you're an oddball, and so you go where you are accepted. It's like the thing of water seeks its own level, and that's true. (052)

From these and other responses, we can see that while it is very common for addicts to reach a point in their careers where they seriously wish to alter their life involvements and stop the use of opiates, they often are confused and uncertain about what course to take. They realize that they share little in common with people in conventional worlds, and because of the stigma of addiction, they are not certain whether others will accept them. To these uncertainties must be added their doubts about whether they *can* actually remain free from opiates.

## Selecting an Alternative to Addiction

When illicit addicts begin to question their lives and resolve to stop using opiates, their change in perspective often is negative in the sense that they see the continued use of opiates, and their involvement with other addicts and the world of addiction, only as undesirable, or worse, as actually or potentially detrimental to their well-being. The change in perspective does not necessarily entail a positive view that could provide an alternative to their present situation. At this point, addicts may know what they do *not* want to do, but they are less certain about what they *do* want.

(Obviously, this predicament does not occur for addicts who drift away from their addiction to participate in social worlds unrelated to the addiction and who maintain the identities and corresponding perspectives rooted in the larger world. Here, the cessation of the addiction is the result of their becoming more immersed in the activities of the non-addictive world and less involved in activities related to the world of addiction. Eventually, the addict behavior dissipates completely.)

Resolving the uncertainties and self-doubts that addicts experience when they are consciously considering giving up their drug use can occur in a number of ways, depending on the alternatives that are fortuitously presented to the addict or deliberately selected by him.

The initial problems that addicts face when they are in the process of stopping the use of the addictive drug are basic, but, depending on the degree to which the addiction has affected an addict's total life scheme, they may seem formidable. Addicts who are seeking to quit their addiction often arrive at this point with scarce social and personal resources. They may have little or no money; they may have no place to live (at least no place that is not tied to the addict world); they may have no friends (except, perhaps, other addicts); and they may feel greatly estranged from their families. Given this situation, addicts must engage in an internal dialogue wherein they consider various options to their predicament until they hit on one that they find personally and socially acceptable, at least for the short run.[3] Some possible alternatives must be excluded because the addicts view them as incompatible with other existing self-images; other alternatives are rejected because they are not thought of as viable. Sometimes the appearance of a workable alternative is a fortuitous matter; the person who is searching for a way out may find it by chance, perhaps through an accidental social encounter.

## Rejection of Treatment

The single option that in some form was available to the large majority of the respondents who recovered naturally was a course of treatment for the addiction. Although nearly all of the study participants considered treatment as a possible alternative, it was eventually rejected by every one of them. The respondents were asked specifically why they did not avail themselves of some form of treatment or seek professional help when they were deciding to stop using opiates. Table 4 provides a summary of their answers.

The table shows that the greatest proportion of the study repondents excluded treatment as an alternative to continu-

3. This decision-making process is similar to the one described by Lemert (1953) that takes place when otherwise conventional, law-abiding people deliberately engage in check forgery.

**Table 4.  Reasons Given for Not Going Into Treatment**

| Reason | Number of Responses |
|---|---|
| No need; thought they could take care of themselves | 35 |
| Did not believe treatment would help | 19 |
| Feared stigmatization (i.e., thought they would be officially recorded as addicts or as mentally ill) | 14 |
| Treatment not readily available | 10 |
| Negative image of treatment programs (methadone just another addiction, cannot identify with other patients, etc.) | 9 |
| Did not wish to be humiliated or degraded | 4 |
| Other | 6 |
| No answer or uncertain | 4 |
| Total | 101 |

ing their addiction because they did not believe they needed formal treatment or because they did not think it would help.[4] One man in the study, addicted to heroin and morphine for five years and not addicted for six years prior to being interviewed, rejected treatment as an alternative because he did not believe he was the kind of person who needed psychiatric help. He recalled:

> It's interesting; it's like I wouldn't want to go to a psychiatrist. I don't need that help because I'm not that kind of person. I'm different from them. (028)

Another respondent, a woman, who had been addicted for

4. The reasons the study participants gave for not seeking treatment when they were deciding to change their lives and give up opiates are very similar to those reported by Tuchfeld (1981) in a study of ex-alcoholics who recovered without treatment.

the relatively short span of eighteen months and who had not been addicted for five years when she was interviewed, explained her reluctance to be treated in terms of a desire to retain her independence.

> I've always been real independent and I guess I had a thing about not needing. I have a real hard time financially being dependent on anybody, you know, anything. I just get . . . I don't want to feel like somebody is going to help me. (094)

The effectiveness of treatment programs also was questioned and was used as a reason not to consider them as possible alternatives by nearly one-fifth of the people studied. A 35-year-old man, who was a high-level and very wealthy heroin dealer, emphasized the ineffectiveness of treatment and, like the woman above, mentioned personal independence. He explained:

> . . . your brain is much more powerful than heroin and that if you want to stop using heroin, I think the best way to stop it is by yourself. I don't think treatment programs, at least not any that I am aware of, work. (085)

Nearly one out of seven respondents in the study rejected treatment as an alternative to their dilemma because they thought they would be stigmatized by being in some way "officially" identified as addicts or identified as being mentally ill. As one young man, who had been addicted for seven years before he quit his drug use, put it:

> I just went in [to a de-toxification center] to see what it was like. The people in there were like losers, like real losers. "Wow, I don't want to get into anything like that." It was terrifying. I thought, "Man, these people are . . . I'd become nuts with these people." That is one of the reasons I don't want help because you go in there and see people like that. (086)

Thus there are several reasons why addicts may shun treatment for their addiction, even though they have resolved to quit using drugs. Whether because of a perceived lack of need, a fear of social stigma, or simply the belief that it would not be helpful, many addicts do not see treatment as a possible way out of their addiction.

## Deliberate and Fortuitous Alternatives

Having excluded treatment as a workable solution to their dilemma, the addicts in the study had proceeded to examine past, current, and possible future relationships and areas to determine whether any of them could provide a way out. This examination entailed the consideration and discarding of possible options—for example, returning to their families or old friends—on the basis of whether they believed the relationships had been ruined, whether bridges to them might be mended, or whether the option was compatible with other existing images of self. Sometimes this internal discussion took a relatively short time—a day or two at the most; in other instances, the process continued for weeks or even months. Not surprisingly, family relationships provided a major pathway for change if the ties to them had not been severed irrevocably. I should note here that families differ greatly in terms of how much untoward behavior they will tolerate before an addict member will be abandoned completely (see also *Proceedings of the Institute on Narcotic Addiction* 1973).

One young man, who had been addicted for nearly two years, recalled how important his family was for him at the time he decided to stop using heroin and change his life.

At the time, my family, man. See, my mother and father always raised me no matter how tough things got. The family is there. No matter how bad it is or how shameful, you can always go back to them. And that's what I did. That's the way we was raised. If we was mad at one another, some shit went down, forget about that shit. I was trying to deal because it was family. I knew I could always go back. I knew a lot of my friends that wanted to kick didn't have no place to go but jail. I remember cats, man, that would be glad to go to jail because at least they are eating a square meal and they could de-tox. So, "Hey, take me, man." That was their family—jail, man. I discovered a lot of people didn't have no place to go. Nowhere. They didn't want to go to jail so they stayed out there in the street life. They stayed out there. But I had a family to go back to, which probably saved my ass. (054)

Another man, who had been addicted for six years, returned to his family's home in a small California town after he encountered serious difficulties in trying to support his habit. He described the importance of his family:

They were very supportive, very supportive. As I said, they were not very wealthy, but they helped me in any way possible. My dad always let me stay there, and he always provided my meals. They just never turned their backs on me. They never threw me out on the streets. Even after some of the things I did. (100)

A second kind of option selected and pursued was one that presented itself by chance and was then chosen after some deliberation. In this situation, the person actively seeks a way out and, perhaps out of desperation, latches on to almost any possibility that presents itself. The fortuitous nature of this pathway can readily be seen in the following recollection of one young woman in the study. She had already resolved to stop using drugs when she had a violent fight with her boy friend, who was also an addict.

He just about killed me! We got into a physical fight, and it had to do with getting high and his guilt and mine. He was a lot bigger than me. I was really small and he really hurt me. I just said, "Forget it," and walked out. I just walked out of the house and never went back. [The next day I went to work] and I felt really badly. I had been out all night walking the streets. I was black and blue around my neck and my face and I had been crying all night. I was really completely a mess. So I went to work and I walked in the door and everybody was there, "What happened to you?" And this one woman, who I didn't hardly know very well at all, we were friendly at work but I didn't know her, said, "Do you need a place to live?" I said, "Yeah." She said, "All right." She just knew I was in a lot of trouble. She helped me out. I felt so separated from my friends. We lived such a secluded life. [It] was really a saving thing for me. And, ah, I don't know, that was it, I moved out. I never got high again after that. (094)

Another respondent, a man who had been addicted to heroin for three and one-half years, told of a conversation he had overheard at his workplace and how, through a combination of chance and later deliberation, it resulted in his abstinence. He recalled:

One day at work, two sisters were talking and one was telling the other about this place, this Transcendental Meditation center. They must have talked for an hour, and I was sitting up there doing my work, but I was listening. So when they finished talking, I got the address and I went down there that same night, and that weekend I started. I knew it would work because there was something in me that made me know that it would work. Plus I had gotten to the point that I felt I was either going to end up OD'ed or in the penitentiary. I mean, any day I was going to be in one of those places. That's how raggedy I was getting. So I started . . . during that time I was trying to stop, like when I was meditating, I just went into it, I just went completely into it. I was meditating right away. I was going through regular withdrawal symptoms and it was hell, but on another level it felt like I wasn't involved in that because I realized one day that I hadn't used in three months! I just started counting it up and three months. And it just blew out my mind. "Thank God!" And I said, "Well, shit, I ain't never going to do it if I went three months! I ain't ever going to do it again in my life!" (045)

The conversation that this man eavesdropped on occurred early in 1971; since he was interviewed in 1979, he had not been addicted for eight years.

## Breaking Away from the Addict World

After the person has tentatively selected an alternative to the addiction, the next step in becoming abstinent is to enact the option. The effort here usually entails literal or symbolic actions taken to sever connections with the addictive drug, with other addicts, and, in general, with the world of addiction. (In this context, literal efforts to move away from the arena of the addict world usually are referred to as attempts at "geographic cures." That is, the addict attempts to stay abstinent by moving away from the place where he was addicted and on to some new geographic area.) The severance of ties to the addictive drug and other addicts can result from voluntary efforts or it can be imposed—for example, through imprisonment. In the latter instance, the formulation of a resolve to stop using may happen when the person is involuntarily abstinent and away from the drug scene. Although the actual attempt at abstinence may start there, however, a test of the strength of the resolve may occur only after the person is released.

Addicts who desire to stop using drugs, but think of themselves as too weak to resist temptations to use again, often believe that they must physically remove themselves from the drug scene if they are to stay with their resolve. This is thought to be especially crucial while they are going through withdrawal, because at that time they are particularly vulnerable to temptations to use the drug once again in order to relieve the withdrawal symptoms. Aside from the temptations presented during the withdrawal period, managing and working through the symptoms of withdrawal do not present most addicts with insurmountable problems. Of course, the severity of withdrawal illness varies with the degree of tolerance that has been developed to the opiate and the method that has been chosen to detoxify. Some addicts elect to wean themselves slowly from the addictive drug, taking smaller and smaller amounts over an extended time. Others stop using abruptly, "cold turkey," and bear the full brunt of the withdrawal. Still others plan in advance for their disengagement and secrete other drugs, such as tranquilizers or barbiturates, for use when they decide to ease the pain of withdrawal. The worst physical symptoms of withdrawal usually pass in three or four days.

Severing one's connections with, and removing oneself from, the drug scene is either relatively simple or very complex and difficult, depending on the resources the addict has and the kinds and exclusiveness of the relationships developed in the drug world. Separating from the drug scene and avoiding other users are not serious problems for relatively isolated addicts who never involved themselves actively with other addicts, except, perhaps, to obtain the drug. They need not concern themselves with problems that other addicts might present for their remaining abstinent, since it is unlikely that other addicts will seek them out or tempt them directly in any way.

Breaking the tie with the addictive drug and the drug world

is much more difficult for addicts who lack the resources and/or the desire physically to remove themselves, in any permanent sense, from areas where drugs are sold and used. The problems of breaking away may be compounded by the ties the addict has to the addict world. Breaking away may also mean dissolving relationships, possibly long-standing ones, with spouses, intimate friends, or lovers who are addicts.

## Symbolic Moving Away

An involuntary removal from the drug scene and then the symbolic separation from it while still remaining in it are well depicted in a story told by a 53-year-old man who had been addicted for more than twenty years. He had decided to change his life and stop using heroin while he was in prison in the state of Washington. He recalled that he could have continued to use heroin in prison, but he decided against it.

> A lot of times in prison my friends from the old neighborhood—they had heroin inside the prison and they offered it to me in different ways. All I had to do was just stick my arm into their cell, through the bars, and then I would get a fix. I reneged on that. I started proving myself. But I still was not sure. I figured that I was okay, but I wanted to prove it to myself when I came back to the neighborhood. That's what I'm proud about; I didn't run from here. I was born and raised in East L.A., and I was going back there. (043)

He was released from prison and returned to Los Angeles. He recalled that he felt strong in his resolve to stay free of heroin, but admitted, "You really don't know until you get out." He obtained employment and soon after moved back into his old neighborhood. He quickly had his resolution tested.

> I got the job and I went to East L.A. to find out for myself where I stand with the guys and everything behind drugs,

and I got a lot of offers [to use heroin]. I told them right off, "No, it's over for me." I wanted to find out for myself. I didn't want to run away from old people that I knew in the neighborhood. [An old friend said], "You son of a bitch, you're really serious about this." I said, "That's right, it's all over." He said, "Don't you crave it?" I said, "I don't think so. I don't want it." He started laughing, and he said, "Okay," and it went right like that. (043)

For this addict, breaking away from the drug world was primarily a symbolic effort. The man returned to the community where he had been addicted, moved regularly among his old drug-using friends, but removed himself from the scene symbolically by presenting himself socially as a nonuser (see Jorquez 1983). Because he did this, other addicts eventually changed their perception of him and no longer responded to him as they would to another addict. At the time the respondent was interviewed, he had not used any drugs since he was released from prison—twelve years before.

Another respondent, a woman who had been addicted to heroin for seven years, also remained in the same community where she had been addicted after she stopped using drugs and symbolically broke away from the world of addiction. Her recovery corresponded with her undergoing a conversion to the Pentecostal church, and she presented herself as a born-again Christian whenever she encountered old friends. She portrayed the change she experienced in herself and the symbolic removal from the world of addiction as follows:

I mean, when I got the Holy Ghost, it spread like wildfire. I'll tell you in fact what happened. You talk about a change. I even answered my phone, "Praise the Lord!" Now can you feature yourself answering the phone, say, "Praise the Lord?" That's how it was, but when I answered it like that it felt so natural. I mean, it was just the most natural thing in the world to me, and it shocked everyone. (005)

In a short time, her addict friends stopped calling her. To which she would no doubt add, "Praise the Lord!"

## Shutting out the Addict World

In spite of the successes of some addicts who leave their geographic area symbolically, other people who are trying to stop their drug use are not certain that they can maintain their resolve to quit and still remain in the company of other addicts. They feel very vulnerable to the temptations of the addict world, yet they do not possess the resources that would enable them to break their ties to that world by moving away. Instead, they attempt to shut themselves off from their old world. For instance, they may lock themselves in their homes and not answer the doorbell or telephone for weeks, venturing outside only when absolutely necessary. The experiences recalled in the following dialogue depict this mode of separation. The woman being interviewed had been addicted for a couple of years, and the addicts in her social circle had come to use her apartment as a gathering place. She did not feel especially strong in her resolve to stop, so she instituted some rather unusual methods to cut the ties with her addict friends. She recalled:

I was getting more secure. The main thing was that I wanted to see how strong I was, and I didn't want to be dependent on anything either. I didn't want to be dependent on drugs if I couldn't get any. I didn't know if I was strong enough to quit [and] it was hard to quit, hard to say no. If somebody came by with drugs to turn me on, it was really hard. So, I just didn't answer the door and I didn't answer the phone. After that, I could cope, but during that time I didn't feel like coping. I felt that there were drugs around and if I was that sick I was naturally going to do them, so I just had to keep everybody out.

*So, did anybody try to break down your door to get in?*

Several times. I thought it was kind of funny. I'd heard one afternoon that somebody was going to try to break in so I put some bacon grease on the fire escape stairs, so if somebody tried to climb up the fire escape and get into my house, they couldn't. (065)

Not all addicts will try to undermine a person's efforts to abstain; in fact, some addicts can be very supportive of such attempts. Nevertheless, the person who is trying to make the break may think it best to get away from the drug world. Often, addicts who are taking their first steps at quitting simply do not wish to run the risk of being tempted and, in a weak moment, fail in their resolve. For whatever reason, if they are not able literally to move away from the area, they may try to shut other addicts out of their lives. Apparently, this strategy can be successful once other users learn that there is nothing to be gained from attempting to maintain the relationship—no loans of money, no drugs, no information of good hustles or good sources of drugs, no companionship.

One man described how his associations with other addicts quickly dissolved after he stopped using.

They stopped coming around because they knew that I didn't have no heroin. I'd wash out my cotton just enough to keep them and then there was no more. [A small piece of cotton is often placed in a container like a spoon. After the drug is heated and dissolved it is drawn through the cotton into a syringe for injection.] So there was no sense in them coming around. They knew that I didn't have nothing to rip off because I'd just come off of heroin. So they just stopped coming around. (017)

## Literal Moving Away

Although symbolic "moves" work for some addicts, the most common way for addicts who are attempting to take the first step to change their lives and sever their ties to the addictive drug and the drug world is to change their environment. Where they move depends on their resources and the existence of positive relationships with nonaddicted friends or relatives. In the description that follows, a woman describes how she moved to Los Angeles to stay with her mother, who was unaware of her addiction. When the addict decided to stop using drugs, she was living in a city north of San Francisco.

> I just got tired of seeing him [her boy friend] going in and sitting and tired of all the money being gone before it really hit me. Everything hit me. I was mad at him and just everything. I just sat down and really thought about it. I had thought the only way I'm going to really get off this stuff is to get away from everyone. I sort of sneakily . . . I disappeared for a year. If I do something, I just more or less do it. That's the only way I could do it. My real mother was down there [in Los Angeles]. I stayed with her for a little while but then I had to get my own place. (020)

Of course, a change in location does not mean, in and of itself, that people will not go back to using addictive drugs. Illicit opiates are available almost everywhere in the United States if someone is inclined to seek them out. Usually, newly abstaining addicts think that by making the drug less available and by minimizing temptations to use, they will increase the chances that they can maintain their resolve to stop. The same woman who is quoted above made the following point about her move to Los Angeles:

> I wanted to [use drugs]. Like I said, I only took a few codeines because I didn't want to use those as a second thing. I wanted to do it completely. I was on MediCal so it would have been easy to go to a doctor, but I didn't, and I really wanted to sometimes. I'm not good at [finding connections]. A lot of people can find a connection anywhere, but I didn't know anybody down there. That's what made me want to go there. I could have taken a plane back to San Francisco and gotten some, but down there I couldn't. (020)

Another respondent, a man who had been addicted for seven years, told a similar story when he moved from the Los Angeles area to northern California. He recalled the reasons why he made the change:

> To get away from it. I left the connections, left the streets, left the junk [heroin]. I was just getting tired of it. I came up here, and I mean there's junk here, but the people, the people you've got to deal with. I can't deal with those people. They're mean. (086)

Still other people make even more drastic moves in their attempts to change their lives and sever their ties to the opiate and the drug world. It is significant that some addicts make a number of changes before they find a location that is sufficiently removed from the world of addiction that they can feel comfortable in their resolve. In the following account, a man addicted for twelve years describes the difficulties he experienced in trying to separate himself from drugs and other addicts. In his first attempt, he moved with his family to a different part of the city in which he had become addicted. They moved into an apartment complex that he was going to manage, but, as he explains, the change just did not work out.

The apartment that we managed, there was a dope dealer living in there. He was selling heroin and everything else. All I had to do was walk out of the door and go over to apartment number whatever it was. So we moved to [Alpine] Lake. I thought that would be ideal and I could get away from the scene. Man, I was running a bit. The way I do it is, I just do it one day at a time or maybe a half-day at a time. So, [Alpine] Lake seemed to be not too far away that we could still keep in contact with the relatives and stuff, but it was just far enough away where it made it a little harder for me to score. (076)

Throughout all these recountings, a common theme can be seen as the addict attempts to stop using drugs: The first step in becoming abstinent is an uncertain one, and it is taken with trepidation. Addicts select an alternative to their lives of addiction on the basis of the options they believe are still available to them and in terms of what they define as personally compatible. In some circumstances, the option that is acted on presents itself fortuitously—a chance social contact, for example, or the sudden renewal of an old friendship. But making the initial break typically involves removing oneself, symbolically or literally, from the drug source, other addicts, and the general world of addiction.

## Problems and Solutions

Once the break with other addicts and the addict world is made, and withdrawal from the addictive drug is complete, addicts are faced with a series of problems revolving around the void in their lives created by the abstinence. No longer does the addict spend a great amount of time each day hustling, obtaining drugs, and using them. In abstinence, ex-addicts usually discover that they have a great deal of time to fill. This may not be a problem for those addicts who never lived almost exclusively in the world of addiction, especially is it not a problem for those who simply drifted away from their addiction and the drug world. They can resume the social relationships and endeavors that were preempted by those activities related to drugs. For most addicts, however, the basic problem in the initial stage of abstinence is what to do with themselves.

One man, who had been addicted for six years, described his initial period of abstinence as similar to that of an alien. Asked what his life was like when he first stopped using opiates, he replied:

> I really didn't start drinking heavily until I actually went to work, making money. I think, if I'm not mistaken, for the first six months I didn't want to go sign up for my unemployment or anything. It would be like if someone kidnapped you and took you to a country where you didn't speak the language, and you had no money, no car, and you were free to come and go as far as you could walk. But you couldn't see your family or friends. Well, heroin addiction, a junkie might look like on the surface that he's living a relatively normal life, except for the use of the drug. Whereas it's a completely different life, like living in a different country. Of course, I was terribly depressed after the physical, initial manifestations of withdrawal disappeared. What you have is a completely vacant life. A giant void there. I can't stress too much the fact that when you're involved with heroin, that's your whole life. You build your whole life on it. You're not concerned with anything except heroin. For the first year [in abstinence] it was like living in a vacuum. There was nothing there I could relate to, nothing I was noticing. (100)

The void created when people stop using addictive drugs and separate themselves from other users commonly is filled by a round of activities that have a single focus. For example, if part of the strategy to establish some distance from the drug corresponds with the ex-addict's becoming a member of a religious group, then daily-life activities focus on religious matters—praying, reading the Bible, attending church services, and the like. If the initial move away from the drug scene happens to correspond with the ex-addict's becoming involved in a political group, then each day centers on political and related activities—a sort of focused immersion. In many instances, the intensity of the involvements and the exclusiveness of them resemble missionary zeal. The all-encompassing nature of the activity is reminiscent of the ex-addict's past behavior with drugs. This intense and highly focused behavior may last for as much as a year after the drug use is stopped.

Another common feature in people's lives during the initial phase of abstinence is the exclusiveness of the social involvements maintained. A kind of moratorium is called on what might be considered a "normal" or conventional round of life activities. There is little, if any, spontaneous or planned venturing out, going beyond the immediate group in which they see themselves as taking part—for example, the family, the church, or the workplace.[5] The reason for this behavior is probably rooted in the uncertainty and anxiety that many new abstainees have about whether nonaddicts will accept them, coupled with their personal doubts that they can stay with their resolve and remain free of drugs. Some addicts simply do not have any relatives or friends to socialize with who are not addicts. At this point, their life stance is

5. As a matter of comparison, it is significant to note that this kind of social separation also is intentionally structured in certain programs set up to treat addicts and alcoholics. For example, it is typical of programs modeled after Synanon, such as Delancy Street and Daytop (see Cassiel and Amen 1971; Yablonsky 1965).

rather conservative; since they are successfully abstaining in their current situation, they believe they should "leave well enough alone."

Thus the focused immersion of ex-addicts in a rather singular round of life that is characteristic of the initial period following withdrawal is often self-imposed. But it may be an artifact of the situation the addict finds himself in, for example, a protracted work schedule. In the account that follows, a man who had been addicted for twenty years describes the singular and intense focus his life took when he stopped using drugs.

> Instead of being a compulsive drug user, I became a compulsive workaholic. I put all my energy into work. I did not go out with a girl for one year. No sex for a year, no drugs. I didn't touch anything. I'd smoke a lot of marijuana. I'd come home from work, I'd sit down and get a half of pizza or some sandwich . . . and I'd get my little pipe. At that time I was making a little money and I could afford to smoke some dope, watch some television, go to sleep. I threw myself almost wholly into not going out to East L.A. and seeing people in the drug culture. I still work six days a week. But Saturday I don't go in until eight o'clock, and I only work until eleven or so. (089)

Another man recalled similar experiences of intensely focused time during the period when he first became abstinent. To get away from the drug scene, he and his wife, who was also an addict, moved from southern California to a rural farming area in the state where he obtained employment milking cows.

> I milked from two to six in the morning. No, from two to seven. It was a ten-hour shift. The morning was a little longer than the evening. Then I'd go home, and that's my sleeping time. I'd get up again at two in the afternoon [and

work] until seven in the evening. So that's the day right there. You have to devote your total twenty-four hours to a one-day shift because your time off is sleeping time. Sometimes I got [my days off] all in a row, four in a row, when he couldn't give them to me once a week. (014)

## The Changing Drug Scene

Gradually, while the individual has literally or symbolically sequestered himself from the drug world and other addicts, changes occur that increase the likelihood that the person will remain abstinent. One of these changes has to do with the drug scene itself. As I noted, because of the illicit status of opiates, the drug scene is very volatile and chaotic. Addict social circles are continually changing and breaking down as various members drift off into other involvements, are arrested and jailed, are hospitalized, or die. Individuals who sever their ties with the addictive drug by moving away from the drug scene typically are surprised when they return to their old haunts by how much things have changed. Old drug-using partners and dealers are no longer around, so people who have been away, even for as brief a time as a few months, may find it harder to obtain drugs than they might have expected. Problems in obtaining the drug may be enough to dissuade abstinent individuals from starting to use drugs again. It simply may be too much bother to find a new connection and not worth the trouble or risk (cf. Scharse 1966). One man in the study described how the drug scene he had been involved with for six years had changed during the year he had been away from it:

The last trip, the last few times I went down there, I tried to score and it was no longer around anymore. I couldn't believe it. The town has changed from the time I was there. Like I said, there was possibly a hundred and fifty people using heroin, maybe fifty in the group that I knew. I know there's still a couple there, but it's just not available. And if it is available, it's terribly expensive. It has gradually become just too much trouble. (100)

Another respondent, a woman who was addicted to heroin during the Flower Children era of the late 1960s, had similar experiences when, after nine months away from the area, she returned to the Haight-Ashbury district in San Francisco. She recalled:

Well what happened was—one good thing was accomplished during the nine months that I was not there—that group of friends that were using didn't know how to get hold of me. I did not let any of them know I was back. A lot of them by that time had left the city themselves and gone in various directions. I no longer had that, "Well, we're going to get some, do you want to go in on it?" type thing. Another thing that was very good, I no longer knew where to get it. I wasn't about to go walk up and down Haight Street. I had no idea where it . . . the few connections that I did have either moved away, ended up in jail or whatever. I wasn't about to just go wandering around searching for it; you never know what you're going to get. (049)

Obviously, the point here is not that the additional difficulties involved in obtaining drugs will effectively dissuade addicts from further use. Rather, the fact is that the absence of ready sources for the drug may make it so hard for a person who is abstaining that he decides that it is too much trouble to obtain the drug. Another significant point here is that some ex-addicts find it too much trouble to get the drug when it is not really all that hard to purchase it.

*Establishing Relationships with Nonaddicts*

When addicts make the initial break with the drug world, they usually are very apprehensive about the future. In addition to not knowing what they are going to do, and whether they can live without opiates, they may question whether they have anything in common with nonaddicts. In the past, addicts may have depicted nonaddicts as "squares," for addicts feel seriously estranged from the conventional world. Some newly abstinent people are in fact so out of touch with the everyday world that they experience great difficulties in doing such ordinary things as going to a supermarket to shop for food or to a laundromat to wash clothes. They may become deeply depressed in the early stages of abstinence (cf. Senay 1983).

These problems usually are resolved over time in the course of remaining abstinent. Individuals become increasingly involved in ordinary social activities once they stop using drugs. Even though at first they develop highly exclusive and focused social involvements to take the place of the activities they engaged in when they were addicted, they are nonetheless undergoing social experiences with nonaddicts. In time, these experiences can provide the basis for a commonality of discourse. Non-drug-related experiences in church work, a political group, or the workplace can create a social background on which to base common interests and everyday interaction. Almost unwittingly, abstaining addicts find that they are accepted in the conventional world, that they can develop new associations, friendships, and interests. (However, as I show later in the book, this acceptance in the nonaddictive world often involves some hardship.) One man described how his feelings of estrangement gradually dissipated over the course of his recovery when he took a job in a business office.

was like, I'd go to work in this office and I would just, in world that I had no experiences in, and all of these people re very straight. The first time it was very traumatic. As a matter of fact, it really felt like I was a wolf among sheep. I really wanted to, you know, go up to some of these people and say, "Look, I need forty dollars until next weekend." It was just such a change from what I had been in that it was incredible. And eventually, it got around to the point where the idea of finding anything more than a McDonald's for dinner and not taking the rest of the money and buying dope with it had always seemed to me to be real prime foolishness. Eventually I had come around to the point where I enjoyed going out with people and just sitting around and talking and picking up my share of the tab. (92)

Another man recalled similar experiences in the course of establishing new relationships with nonaddicts.

I didn't go to any special places to change friends. Things just flowed naturally to other people. I met new friends through work mainly and going out. I didn't go to bars. Basically, it was through people at work. You know, you're with them enough hours of the day to tell if you really like them or not, rather than just meeting someone on the street and saying, "Come on over for dinner and maybe we'll be friends." That's not the way to do it. It has to come through other channels and then maybe meet somebody through those people. (101)

Some of the untreated, ex-addicts in the study found it necessary to conceal their past lives from the new people they associated with after breaking with the addict world. Usually, the concealment was motivated by fears that they would not be accepted if their pasts were known. In a few instances, respondents even refused to sign their names to the study's informed-consent sheet, fearing that the information might somehow become public and affect their lives negatively. Other ex-addicts, in contrast, were quite open about the past, sometimes even exploiting their lives as addicts, as, for example, by becoming drug-abuse counselors.

## Emerging Stakes in Staying Abstinent

As abstaining addicts continue to keep apart from the drug world and continue to associate with and feel accepted by nonaddicts, they develop a growing sense of confidence that they can, in fact, live without opiates. In the course of remaining abstinent from the drug and associating with conventional others, a strong social-psychological commitment not to return to using opiates may develop (see Becker 1960). This commitment generally is related to the addicts' present relationships and the corresponding identities, interests, and investments that they define as incompatible with opiate use. Some individuals may still talk favorably about the euphoric effects of the drug they were addicted to, but they do not return to using it. In part, this is because of the new risks involved. Addicts who make the break from the drug world may develop new commitments to people they care for and love, may invest time and effort in new careers, and may acquire skills or obtain things of value to them that they do not wish to lose. As they remain abstinent, they develop a stake in their new lives that is incompatible with opiate use and addicts. In their abstinent state they have too much to lose to go back to using opiates.

The woman quoted earlier in this chapter who moved from San Francisco to stay with her mother in Los Angeles later obtained welfare support and moved into her own apartment with her son. She stayed pretty much to herself, caring for her son and reading. After about a year in her new life, she visited San Francisco. She recalled what took place:

I tested myself by coming back to San Francisco. I really did. You know, I was kind of scared because I thought as soon as I see my girl friends and stuff, "Oh, you have got to get loaded." But I didn't. I couldn't believe it. I really could believe myself because I thought if I get loaded once, then I'm going to want to move back up here and it's going to start all over again. I've worked too hard for a year, and I'm not going to blow it. (020)

She had a stake in her new life involvements that she did not want to jeopardize by becoming a user again. Returning to San Francisco was a test of the strength of her resolution to remain abstinent. Apparently her test was successful, for she had not been readdicted for two and one-half years when she was interviewed.

Another respondent, who had been addicted over a period of twenty years, told how the development of new stakes in different aspects of his life worked to help him remain free of opiates. He described how new opportunities emerged in his life:

I became a partner in a business. The business grew, and we changed its focus a little bit. Building a company is satisfying. I had achievement on achievement from it. That's good. It's nice to see it grow. It's nice to be alive without every damn dime I earn as a human being [going to drugs]— this is the first time in a long, long time that I ever had a significant cash flow, a nice home—a nice stable home situation where the phone wasn't ringing off the hook. Come sell me this, come buy me this. My wife is not out being a whore. I'm not dealing with crazy people. This is the first time in twelve years I've had a stable home. I've got a nice life, and I look forward to coming home. I met a nice girl. We're going to get married. She's a very sweet, nice person. I have a very good sex life. I'm not dissatisfied with my job.

I don't dislike myself. I have too much to lose. If you're a piece of shit drug user in Los Angeles, what's to lose? (089)

The thread that runs through these and other responses is that it is common for addicts, in the course of remaining abstinent, to develop new relationships, interests, and investments that they do not want to risk losing by using drugs again. These new stakes function as strong symbolic wedges and work to continue the separation of the ex-addict from the world of addiction.

**Summing Up**

Addicts who come to a point where they resolve to abstain from the further use of opiate drugs often are uncertain about what they should do with their lives instead. The perspective that commonly accompanies the resolve to quit, when it is coupled with some especially disturbing personal event, usually is negative; that is, the life of addiction now is seen in a negative light, but the change in perspective does not necessarily entail an alternative perspective detailing some other line of action that might be pursued. This problem is more perplexing for those whose lives have been immersed in the world of addiction; they may feel they have nowhere to turn, since they have ruined most of the conventional social relationships in their lives. In contrast, addicts who have not lived solely in the addictive world may have an easier time, at least initially, in realizing their goal by turning to some relationship that has not been destroyed or by mending a bridge to one that has not been damaged beyond repair.

The initial step in breaking away from drug addiction typically involves a literal or symbolic move away from the drug itself and the drug world. Following the period of withdrawal, addicts face the basic problem of filling the time in their lives that once was taken up with hustling, finding, purchasing, and using the drug. Whatever activities fill the void—work, child care, religion, politics, or physicial exercise—become almost the exclusive focus of the addict's life and are fervently performed. During this time, which typically lasts about a year, a moratorium takes place on what might be considered a "normal" round of life. The abstaining individual rarely ventures beyond the safe confines of the group or activities with which he is engrossed.

Other important changes also take place during the initial months following separation from the drug world. First, the drug scene itself may become less familiar to the addict. Old drug-using friends and dealers leave the area, some may go to jail or into treatment, and some may die. Such changes make it more difficult for abstainers to obtain the drug, should they be tempted to do so. (Of course, to anyone who is intent on obtaining a drug, the altered drug scene will not, in and of itself, prove to be much of a deterrent.) Second, in the course of staying abstinent, ex-addicts undergo experiences that they can and do share with nonaddicts. After a while, these experiences establish the groundwork for a commonality of discourse, and once it occurs, it helps abstaining addicts to overcome their fears that they cannot get along with nonaddicts because they will not be accepted by them. Concomitantly, ex-addicts begin forging new affiliations with conventional people, possibly developing intimate relationships, building a family, and acquiring a liking for material things and the comparative security of a drug-free life. Finally, the abstaining addicts may develop personal stakes in their new life involvements and may not wish to jeopardize them by returning to the drug. These new stakes can serve as wedges to help continue the separation of the abstainers from the drug world and its participants. And where the decision to stop using drugs was centered in some problem directly related to the drug world (e.g., having committed a robbery or informed on a drug dealer), returning to the drug world may be made more unlikely because of the personal danger involved.

The social relationships, interests, and investments that develop in the course of abstinence reflect the gradual emergence of new identities and corresponding new perspectives. Now the abstaining individuals know not only what they do *not* want to do but also what they *would* like to do and become. They can begin to plan and work for a future unrelated to drugs.

# 4
## Staying Abstinent

> [Craving drugs is] . . . a good feeling. It just crosses your
> mind at times. Sometimes an urge to fix [inject the drug]
> comes from no apparent reason . . . the appetite just comes
> out. (038)

Thoughts such as these often appear, uninvited, to ex-
addicts. People who have been addicted to opiate drugs report
experiencing cravings for drugs long after they have physically withdrawn from them. Craving experiences have be-
wildered both those who have undergone them and professionals who study addiction. Addicts who have returned to
using addictive drugs following voluntary attempts at abstinence regularly attribute their relapses to the "craving phenomenon." Correspondingly, many theories of addiction—
particularly opiate addiction and alcoholism—propose that
the craving phenomenon is especially important in explaining the processes of relapse and readdiction following periods of abstinence. Although many different words have been
used in the literature to refer to the phenomenon (e.g., crave,
yen, desire, impulse, urge, and need), they are generally used
interchangeably to designate an emotional and cognitive
state experienced by abstaining addicts as an impulse—a
strong need or desire to use opiates again (Chein 1964; Dole
and Nyswander 1967; Lindesmith 1968; Rubington 1978;
Taylor and Lantinga 1979; Wikler 1953, 1965, 1973).

The continued existence and possible activation of the
craving phenomenon is seen as a harbinger of renewed drug

use and consequent readdiction. A major problem, then, for people who have stopped their addictive use of opiates or alcohol is to manage and overcome the cravings they experience to use the drug again. In this chapter I present a description and analysis of the craving phenomenon and how it was managed by the study respondents.

Given the importance attributed to the craving phenomenon for understanding the perplexing tendency of people who have stopped using opiates in an addictive manner to relapse and become readdicted, it is surprising how little is known about the phenomenon. In this context, it is curious that one story frequently told among drug researchers concerns what happens to some people who were once addicted to opiates when they recall and discuss certain aspects of their past lives as addicts. The story proceeds in this fashion: Usually, when in the course of an interview the discussion turns to the amount and quality of the drugs the ex-addicts once used, the respondents begin to act as if they are actually "high" on an opiate drug. They slowly close their eyes, slump over momentarily in a nodding posture, and then, after a few seconds, snap themselves back to an erect position, open their eyes, and attend once more to the discussion. This kind of "nodding behavior" frequently is observed when addicts, intoxicated from an opiate, experience one of its euphoric effects. Although such research incidents apparently are important enough to be recalled and retold in research circles, they rarely are treated as data. Most often, they are simply disregarded, with some reference to the power of suggestion. Unfortunately, attributing such behavior to "suggestion" explains little or nothing.

When ex-addicts exhibit physical symptoms associated with being high on drugs, and this occurs in the midst of discussing the quality and amount of the opiates they once used, a number of questions should arise. Is it a "put on"? Are the respondents only acting as if they feel high, or do they actually feel high? Does such a state show a "need" for the drug? Are they experiencing a craving? Or does the physical state that resembles opiate intoxification have to be coupled with cognitions—thoughts—about obtaining and actually using the drug before it can be defined as a craving or need? Whatever the truth of the matter, this research anecdote provided part of the initial impetus in this study to explore the nature of drug cravings as they were experienced and described by the respondents.

## Theories of the Craving Phenomenon

### Learned Associations with Withdrawal Distress

There are a number of theories concerning the nature and effects of the craving phenomenon, and although the differences between them may seem to be splitting hairs and even irrelevant, the variations may be very important in terms of their implications. Lindesmith (1968), in his classic work on opiate addiction, makes what is probably one of the strongest statements concerning the relationship between drug cravings and consequent relapse. He maintains that certain opiate-related attitudes that are socially engendered in the early stages of drug use tend to develop an independent status and subjectively persist through extended periods of abstinence, even after the physiological conditions of the addiction have long since passed. Because of past experiences that people had while addicted, in using the opiate to ward off the onset of withdrawal symptoms, they learn to generalize withdrawal distress and come to use the drug in response to all forms of stress. When people are abstinent from the drug, they experience "stress" as a craving to use the addictive drug once again.

Lindesmith contends that the acquired attitudes—related initially to the use of opiates to avoid withdrawal distress and in later opiate use a response to all forms of stress—are latent during periods of abstinence, but under certain conditions can reemerge and be experienced as strong impulses or cravings to use the drug again. These cravings act as precursors to renewed drug use and consequent readdiction. As long as the opiate-related attitudes are retained, Lindesmith maintains, abstaining addicts cannot be said to be recovered or cured. According to Lindesmith, people who retain such attitudes, even if they have not used an addictive drug for many years, must still be considered addicted, for relapse may occur at any time. The strength of Lindesmith's position concerning the unlikelihood that addicts might recover can be seen in the following statement: ". . . it is agreed by all who have studied them [opiate addicts] in any part of the world that relapse rates are high and that the impulse to relapse is probably permanent and ineradicable" (Lindesmith 1968, 53). People who never learn to associate the use of the drug with avoidance of withdrawal distress, maintains Lindesmith, should not be considered addicted but merely habituated.

## Conditioned Associations with Withdrawal Distress

Another widely cited explanation of the relationship between cravings and relapse is the view formulated by Wikler (1953, 1965, 1973). He takes the position that the relapse of abstaining opiate addicts can be attributed to conditioned withdrawal sickness. People who have stopped using opiates will crave the drug and possibly become readdicted if they are exposed to certain stimuli that they have learned, as a result of their past experiences with withdrawal sickness, to associate with actual acute withdrawal. For example, on returning to neighborhoods where they once obtained and used opiates, abstaining individuals may experience such symptoms of withdrawal as a runny nose and muscle pain; as a result of these feelings, they may begin to think about the addictive drug, obtain and use it, and thus, possibly, relapse. According to Wikler, individuals react to these symptoms as they once did to the actual discomfort of withdrawal by craving for and using the drug to relieve the unpleasant condition. (For a recent test of Wikler's hypothesis, see McAuliffe forthcoming.)

Focusing on the problem of alcoholism, Rubington's research (1978) on the craving phenomenon led him to make a distinction between craving and an abstinent individual's thinking about a drink. Rubington maintained that thinking about a drink is a cognitive or psychic event, whereas craving a drink is a physical experience (also see Isbell 1955). Presumably, one can experience the two states independently or concurrently. Although this distinction may be a true one, its importance for understanding relapse among people who are abstaining from alcohol is not clear. It is questionable whether a person can experience cravings *for alcohol* without subjectively defining the meaning of the feeling. That is, if the person is going to direct his behavior to obtain and use alcohol, the physical experience must first be *defined* as a *craving for alcohol*. In contrast, one can think about drinking without experiencing a corresponding physiological craving state.

McAuliffe and Gordon (1974, 1981) reexamined the nature of cravings as they related to opiate addiction and presented a theory that offers a partial reconceptualization of the phenomenon. They were in agreement with those theorists who felt that cravings can result in the relapse of persons abstaining from the use of opiates but that the reason for the relapse—cravings—can be a desire to experience once again the euphoric effects of the drug. Cravings are not seen as resulting exclusively from conditioned associations with withdrawal sickness or as the result of generalizing the symptoms of withdrawal distress to all forms of stress. McAuliffe and Gordon suggest that at least some people who are abstaining can relapse and become readdicted because, under certain conditions, they crave the euphoria produced by opiates—they simply like the "high" that they experience when they use the drug.

We have, then, several competing theories of addiction and relapse and a number of definitions of the craving phenomenon. These theories and definitions serve as a backdrop as we now compare and contrast craving experiences as they were described and managed by the ex-addicts in this study.

### Respondent Experiences with Withdrawal Distress

All the people included in this study had ample experience when they were addicted to learn to associate their use of opiates with the avoidance of withdrawal distress or sickness. They also experienced the euphoric effects of the addictive drug.

To be included in the study, potential respondents had to have been addicted for at least one year. As I noted in the first chapter, most of the people selected for the study (73 respondents) had been addicted for three years or longer. The average period of addiction for the entire group was five years and eight months (5.69 years). The person addicted for the longest time, a man, had been addicted over a period of thirty years.

Another criterion that potential respondents had to meet to qualify for the research was related to the withdrawal symptoms they had experienced. During a screening interview, respondents were asked to describe the symptoms that they had undergone during episodes when they had withdrawn from the addictive drug without any formal detoxification treatment. To be accepted, the ex-addicts had to mention voluntarily at least five of ten symptoms commonly associated with physical withdrawal from an addiction to an opiate drug. The frequency with which they mentioned each of the ten symptoms is presented in Table 5. Seventy-one respondents, more than seven out of ten, recalled having experienced at least seven of these symptoms during a period of withdrawal.

It would seem reasonable to conclude that the length of time over which the respondents reported to have been addicted and the self-reports of the various withdrawal symptoms they had experienced are sufficient to provide an adequate data base for comparison with what some existing theories of addiction would predict concerning the nature and consequences of the craving phenomenon. That is, the overall length of the addiction and the experiences of withdrawal are of adequate duration and intensity to have estab-

**Table 5.   Withdrawal Symptoms Reported by Study Respondents**

| *Symptom* | *Frequency of Mention (%)* |
|---|---|
| Chills | 93 |
| Runny eyes and nose | 93 |
| Trouble sleeping | 91 |
| Sweating and flushed skin | 90 |
| Pain in muscles | 82 |
| Stomach cramps | 75 |
| Nausea | 74 |
| Muscle twitching | 68 |
| Diarrhea | 60 |
| Headaches | 55 |

lished in the mind of the user an association between the use of the opiate and the distress of withdrawal, or with the various cues related to withdrawal sickness, if such associations are going to occur at all.

## Managing the Craving Phenomenon

Many of the respondents who could recall experiences that they defined as a craving to use opiate drugs once more identified the source of the desire as something that they associated in the past with using the drug and not withdrawing from it.[1] This is contrary to what would be predicted from the theories of Lindesmith and Wikler. Moreover, the direction of the desire and the bodily feelings that the respondents described as having experienced at the moment of the craving were both more often defined in positive terms of wanting to get "high" than in terms related to withdrawal distress or sickness.

### Environmental Cues

Those in the study who were able to isolate the source of their cravings to use drugs again usually pointed to some olfactory or visual cue that they associated in their past experiences with obtaining the drug and/or using it. Being in an area where they once had obtained the drug, seeing old addict associates, or (especially) witnessing another person use drugs were the most frequently reported events that en-

---

1. In this chapter I am unable to report the relative numbers of all the respondents who identified or defined their craving experience in different ways. This omission is the result of two factors: (1) Specific exploration of the phenomenon and its importance did not occur to me until the research was well along; and (2) the respondents differed greatly in terms of their ability to recall whether they had experienced cravings and how well they could articulate their feelings if they could recall them.

gendered cravings to use opiates. One man, who had been addicted over a period of twelve years and not addicted for five years prior to his being interviewed, recalled how drug cravings were prompted when he saw a group of actors seem to inject heroin in a movie that he was watching on television:

> Like, yesterday, just yesterday, I was watching *Who'll Stop the Rain?* It was on the movie channel, right? and I hadn't seen it at the movies and I was watching it in my room. And they had this one scene where they were all shooting up, right? I'm sitting there and I'm going, "Ahhhh . . . I don't need this!" And I was thinking that it was pretty real, they're doing a pretty good scene. You sit there and you see everybody, and Tuesday Weld, she's having a nervous breakdown and they give her a little to calm her down and she goes, "Ahhh." And I'm here thinking, "I never had anything that good. Ever!"
>
> *So you have had cravings?*
>
> Yeah, for heroin. (035)

The man who was quoted briefly at the beginning of this chapter explained that he often felt a craving to use when he was in areas where he had once obtained the drug:

> *You said that even today you have to deal with the cravings, wanting to get down [use heroin]. Tell me about today, what are you talking about?*
>
> Well, when you get loaded, it's a good feeling. I don't know, it just crosses your mind at times. Sometimes an urge to fix comes from no apparent reason. It crosses your mind like either from cruising through a neighborhood and seeing where a dude [a dealer] lives or knowing where a dude lives. The appetite comes out. (038)

Olfactory cues were also reported to stimulate cravings to use opiates. With these cues, the cravings resulted from associations made with some aspect of the event of using the drug, with the immediate effects of the drug, and/or with settings where the drug typically was used. The smell of urine or vomit occasionally was reported to stimulate cravings. These odors are associated either with the practices of using the drug in the privacy of a restroom or with the almost customary experience of voiding the stomach's contents as an immediate reaction to the drug. The smell of sulfur released by burning matches was also reported to stimulate cravings. This association is related to the practice of dissolving illicit heroin in water and heating it with matches in a small container, such as a spoon or bottle cap, before it is drawn into a syringe and injected. The lasting power of this particular association was well described by a woman who had been addicted for close to six years and had not been addicted for nearly fourteen years at the time she was interviewed. She explained how the odor of a burned match still affected her:

> It was, as I said, something that has never left me that is associated with heroin. To this day, when a stick match is lit and I smell the sulfur burn afterward, I immediately react like when you are taking off [injecting heroin]. I get that warm feeling, the muscles tighten, and I get a small rush coming up. I still have it. There is that brief second of that good, nice feeling of getting high. I have never gotten rid of that. Any time I get that sulfur match smell— (011)

A rather unusual association between an olfactory stimulus and a craving for heroin was described by another respondent. At the time he was interviewed, he had not been addicted to opiates for three and a half years. After he explained that occasionally he did experience cravings to use drugs again, he was asked to describe what it was like. He replied:

> Ah . . . when I get it, it's not unpleasant. It's like if you

were sitting around and said, "Gee, I have the urge to have a chocolate." Well, maybe it happens once a month. I'll be sitting around and all of the sudden I'll smell heroin. It's got a particular smell to it. Sweet, very sweet. It's like a gardenia, almost. Nothing like it. It's not quite that sticky sweet, but it's sort of a little bit saltier. Some people taste it, I smell it. But, like, when it's surging through the bloodstream . . . at any rate, I'll just smell it, just out of the blue, and it'll stay with me for about five minutes to a half-hour or an hour. (087)

The nature of cravings to use opiate drugs after having managed to stop using them varies with different people. Undeniably, some of the respondents who reported an occasional craving once again to use opiate drugs described the source of the inclination in terms that broadly could be interpreted as a generalization of experiences related to withdrawal distress or a conditioned response to cues associated with withdrawal sickness. Typically, in these instances, the respondents believed the source of the cravings was rooted in feelings of depression or stress; individuals remembered how the drug had helped to ameliorate such unpleasant states in the past.

One young man explained how sometimes he thought about using drugs again when he was depressed:

Yeah, I still get them, especially when I'm feeling very low and depressed—rejected. Then I want to go out and chip [use the drug]. So I go out and smoke weed, have a few cocktails. It helps. [The cravings come] just off the wall. When something bugs me wrong, I say, "The hell with it." Sometimes it's a week and sometimes it's six months. I don't know, it just depends on the time and the circumstances and the place and everything. They are all balled up together. (017)

Another respondent, a woman, also located the source of the cravings in particularly deep depressions. She was asked, "In all the years since you've been clean, have you ever had the urge to use?" She answered:

> Yeah, a couple of times when I got really depressed. I'd think, I'd like to go out and get some stuff, but I didn't do it. [The last time was] maybe six months ago when my husband left. (015)

Although some respondents who had experienced cravings to return to the use of opiates described the source of the inclination in terms that broadly could be interpreted as being related to their having endured withdrawal distress and sickness in the past, their number was relatively small. Moreover, the feeling states that they reported as stimulating thoughts about using drugs once again were rooted in problematic life situations that the respondents were facing at the time. They did *not* report experiencing any specific symptoms of withdrawal distress or illness at the time the cravings occurred.

### Defining and Locating Craving Experiences

Although the phenomenon of craving opiates during periods of nonuse has received a good deal of attention, especially in theories attempting to explain the relapse problem, very little consideration has been devoted to describing or analyzing how cravings feel and how they are defined by persons experiencing them. The experience of any feeling or emotion entails a process wherein the person actively attends to the sensation, defines it, and manages it in some way (Lindesmith, Strauss, and Denzin 1975; see also Hochschild 1975). The manner in which feeling sensations are defined and processed is learned and differs from one person to another on the basis of culture, language group, and social experience. As a result, there is likely to be some variation in how the feeling of cravings to use opiates are described. Some addicts may learn to define anxiety or depression under certain conditions as eliciting a craving to use opiates; others may feel very well when the cravings appear, regardless of the specific stimuli.

Aside from those instances when the cravings were associated with feelings of depression or anxiety that were situated in a life problem, the study respondents who were able to recall and relate the feelings they experienced as cravings generally defined them positively rather than negatively, as Lindesmith and Wikler would predict. The feeling of the cravings commonly was described as akin to actually being high on the drug or as similar to the pleasure of the "rush" that sometimes is felt at the moment the drug is injected.[2] For some individuals, the pleasurable aspects of the craving sensations were followed or accompanied by feelings of nausea, which also are similar to the sensations that addicts report to have felt directly after they inject an opiate. Among those respondents who were able to locate the crave feelings in some part of the body, the throat and abdomen—the stomach in particular—were the areas mentioned most often. The duration of the cravings was relatively short lived; usually they were reported to last fifteen to twenty minutes, sometimes for an hour, and rarely for more than an hour. The frequency with which the cravings occur diminishes over time and generally, after about a year following withdrawal, cravings were reported to appear only rarely, if at all. (On this last point, see also McAuliffe and Gordon 1981.)

The similarity between the pleasurable feeling of the

2. The "rush" seems to be associated more with the use of heroin than the use of such opiates as morphine; however, what actually causes the feeling is not clearly understood. On this point, see Brecher 1972 and Martin and Fraser 1961.

"rush" that sometimes accompanies an intravenous injection of an opiate, particularly heroin, and the craving sensation occasionally experienced when not using drugs was specifically noted by some respondents. One man, who had been addicted to heroin for four years and not addicted for the six years prior to the interview, was asked how frequently he experienced cravings. He observed:

> Oh, irregularly. Infrequently. There's a certain feeling you get in the front of your forehead, like when you're getting your rush, that occasionally I'll experience. I don't know if it's the remnants or some old nerve path or . . . but all of a sudden I'll go, "Hey, I remember that feeling," and it's so weak that it's almost, you have to concentrate on it. Keep it and hold it for a second and I'll think, you know, "It wouldn't be terrible to just go out and cop a bag and take a snort now and then." (092)

Another man also described the similarity between the "rush" sensation and cravings. He was asked, "Since you stopped using, have you ever had times when you've said, 'Oh, it would feel good to "get down" [use drugs] again?'" He explained:

> Not in the sense that I would beat it psychologically, no. The sensation of the feeling of the rush once you inject yourself directly into the mainline and for a few seconds you get this rush—that feeling maybe—but not the dependency that I would feel in trying to overcome some kind of situation. [Then] it just goes away. Right now, I guess, the same is when I have a feeling of wondering what it would be like to have a fix again—it just goes away. I'll think, "Well, not me anymore!" I'll probably feel nauseated. I get a nauseated thing, you know. The nauseating thing is actually, in the subculture, interpreted as being a desirable thing to feel. But I don't feel that way anymore. (012)

Nausea, often felt as a sensation of impending vomiting, is usually described as a feeling of sickness centered in the stomach and throat. Not surprisingly, the ex-addicts in the study who located the feeling of their cravings in some part of the body commonly situated it in the upper gastrointestinal system, specifically in the stomach and/or the general area of the throat. The identification of one of the crave feelings as nausea and the locating of it in the gastrointestinal system does not seem to be associated with withdrawal distress or sickness, as the theories of Lindesmith or Wikler claim. Rather, the crave feelings are specifically related to using opiates and the immediate pleasurable effects of the "rush" and the "high." In addition, the two withdrawal symptoms reflecting these feelings—the experience of stomach cramps and nausea—were among the five symptoms mentioned *least* often by the study participants (see Table 5). Locating the cravings in the stomach area is clearly illustrated in the dialogue that follows. The discussion occurred during the group interview described earlier. The nature of the craving phenomenon was being discussed, and one participant described his experiences:

> I know that I would have feelings that would wrench my gut. I would feel a rush all over my body, particularly in my stomach . . . in my arm. I would just rub my arm. There was all that to it, yet I would try to direct my mind elsewhere and try to think of other things.

> *Was it an emotional thing or a physical thing?*

> The craving was both. It had both physical manifestations and a sense of tension throughout my limbs and everything and also my stomach was tied up in knots. But also the emotional aspect of the feeling, an extreme desire, the wanting, I don't know how to characterize that, but sure, there is an emotional aspect. (Group interview)

Although the "tension" described by this man could be interpreted as a feeling associated with the distress of withdrawal or illness, he described it in the context of a "rush"—that is, an immediate effect of using opiates and not as part of withdrawing from them.

A woman respondent recalled that she experienced cravings when she smelled the odor of sulfur from a burned match. She was asked whether the feeling was euphoric. She answered:

> Yes, it's very warm, good. . . . My stomach would tighten and I would get that warm feeling coming up my esophagus. (011)

Another respondent, a 36-year-old man, likened himself to one of Pavlov's dogs when he felt the nausea accompanying a craving. He explained:

> I had the objectivity to even see my own behavior for what it was and that was like getting nauseous whenever I'd even think about fixing. Like one of Pavlov's dogs. I don't consider myself a neurotic person and I was doing some really wimpy shit.
>
> *Was it like the nausea people get when they use?*
>
> Yeah, it was the same kind of nausea . . . that you get when you use. Some people get sick when they smell a match. I've seen that. (032)

Still another respondent, a young woman, described the symptoms of her cravings in terms of nausea and centered them in her throat. She was asked whether she ever experienced cravings, and she replied:

> Yeah, a few weeks ago.
>
> *What did it feel like?*
>
> It felt, I felt the craving—I felt saliva.

*Did your mouth water?*

Yeah. And my throat kind of closes up. And I started sneezing. And then I started getting nauseated. I usually get nauseated and then I get a headache and then I get over it.

*Okay, how long does it last?*

It can last sometimes for an hour, or it can last like fifteen minutes.

*What's the longest?*

Probably not longer than forty-five minutes to an hour [and the shortest] about ten minutes. (034)

Other researchers also have reported instances where people situated the feeling they associated with cravings in the stomach area. Lindesmith related the following incident: After he had finished delivering a paper about addiction at a professional meeting, a man from the audience approached him and described the cravings he felt that afternoon when the drug was being discussed. Lindesmith reported that he asked the man what exactly it was that he felt, and the man explained that he "broke into a cold sweat and felt a peculiar sensation in the pit of his stomach" (1968, 132). In spite of these feelings, the man said that "he had been gripped by a powerful 'yen' to have a shot of the drug that was being talked about so much." The man associated the cravings with the drug and with using the drug; nevertheless, the craving was attributed to withdrawal symptoms.

Similar instances have been reported in the clinical literature. Taylor and Lantinga, in a paper detailing the use of a therapeutic technique for "urge reduction" in substance users, describe a man who had fixed the feeling of his drug cravings in his chest and stomach. "For Jim, the urge consisted mainly of a cognitive image of 'scoring, fixing, and getting off,' accompanied by sensations of tension in his chest and stomach" (1979, Appendix B).

*Time and the Diminishment of Cravings*

Respondents who remembered having experiences resembling cravings to use opiates again after they had stopped their drug use generally recalled that the events came about most frequently during the first year of their abstinence (see McAuliffe and Gordon 1981). As time passed and they stayed with their resolve not to use the addictive drug, and as they involved themselves in activities unrelated to illicit opiates, the moments in which they felt cravings grew less and less frequent. In fact, a few respondents claimed that they never felt any need or craving to use drugs again once they had broken their addiction.

Although a few people in the study said that they still experienced cravings for opiates many years after they had stopped their addictive use of them, the cravings now appeared only rarely, rather than with the frequency of appearance that characterized the first year of abstinence. It is difficult to say whether the frequency of the cravings actually diminished significantly at the end of a year's time or whether the respondents were simply using a convenient category to mark the point where they remembered the cravings as no longer presenting serious problems for them. In any event, most of the study participants who could remember the cravings reported that they did decrease significantly, both in frequency and strength, after about a year of abstinence.

One woman, who had not been addicted for seven years when she was interviewed, described the point when she stopped craving the drug. In the following dialogue, she is explaining how she currently felt about heroin.

You know, dope doesn't worry me anymore. Dope doesn't enter my mind anymore.

*Do you get cravings or urges?*

Oh, no. During the first—I would say about the first year after I actually kicked that last time—well, I would feel it now and then. I would think about it hard. (078)

Another respondent, a 30-year-old man who had been addicted to heroin for almost two years and had not been addicted for four and a half years when he was contacted for the study, described how vulnerable he felt in the first year of abstinence. He was asked: "How long did it take before you really knew you were going to make it?" He replied:

A whole year.

*You felt shaky that whole year?*

A whole year.

*Did you have cravings a lot?*

Heroin, yeah, for damned near six months. (054)

Still another man described how his "compulsion" to use opiates gradually dissipated when he stopped using drugs. After he broke away from the heroin scene, he moved to a small town in the Sierra Nevada where he and his family lived for the next thirteen months. He was asked if he occasionally used heroin during that period. He responded:

No, I didn't.

*But you were thinking about using all the time?*

Yes.

*It was on your mind?*

Yeah.

*You would dream about it?*

Yeah, I would dream at night, I'm sure every addict does, that I was fixing up.

*What happened when you moved?*

. . . it was really a blessing that we could get away from

there [the drug scene]. We lived in a little bitty trailer about as big as this kitchen. But I wouldn't have cared if it was half that big. I got away from it by moving and then as the days went by I didn't really have that compulsion so much. (076)

In addition to these accounts of the craving phenomenon, the ex-addicts in this study show that thoughts of once again using opiates do arise when the person is experiencing some stress or is depressed—that is, cravings are loosely associated with withdrawal distress or sickness. However, cravings also are clearly related to past experiences with the drug's euphoric effects. In fact, a close examination of the cues reported to give rise to thoughts of using and the feelings that ex-addicts report to have experienced at the time shows that the cravings are related to things associated in the past, either with using the drug or with its immediate effects.

If we concluded that the craving phenomenon was associated exclusively with withdrawal distress or illness, we would expect respondents to report that they had felt some of the symptoms of withdrawal distress or illness during the crave experience. Yet the only frequently recalled feeling that could be thought of as a symptom of withdrawal—the feeling of nausea—also is known to be one of the immediate effects of opiate drugs on the body. Even the cold sweat reported by the ex-addict in the case cited by Lindesmith could as easily be taken to be an indication of the effect of an opiate on the body as it could be an indication of withdrawal. That is, opiate drugs—especially morphine—are known to decrease the responses of the part of the brain called the hypothalamus to external input. This lowered response impairs the brain's regulation of homeostatic functions; for example, body temperature decreases following the administration of the drug (Ray 1978), which could account for the cold sweat in the case reported by Lindesmith.

To reemphasize, the feelings that the respondents reported

having during the moment of a craving very often were described in the positive terms generally associated with the euphoric effects of opiate drugs, rather than in terms that might be associated exclusively with withdrawal distress or sickness. The actual feeling of the craving experience commonly was described as "very warm and good," or as being "like the feeling of the 'rush' you get when you inject" the drug. Clearly, it would be difficult to interpret such descriptions as in any way related to distress or illness.

One further point should be mentioned here. It may be more than coincidental that the crave symptoms described by the ex-addicts in the study closely resemble some of the known pharmacological effects of narcotics such as morphine. For example, a few of the most widely cited "adverse reactions" to morphine noted in pharmacology textbooks are nausea, vomiting, anorexia (the lack of appetite), and constipation (Jaffe 1970; Ray 1978). The nausea and vomiting result from morphine's effect on the lower brain areas that control these actions. Morphine also affects the gastrointestinal system, impairing digestion by lowering the secretion of digestive fluids and slowing the movement of foodstuffs by decreasing the number of peristaltic contractions in the intestines. These actions bring about anorexia and constipation, and may be related to some of the craving symptoms described by the study respondents.

Perhaps people who undergo cravings for opiates after they stop using them are actually experiencing a low-grade, physiological "high," which they identify as being like the effects of opiates they have used. As I mentioned briefly in the first chapter, recent discoveries in biochemical research have led some scientists to speculate about the existence of opiate-like substances that are naturally manufactured in the body. These biochemical substances, called *endorphins*, are hypothesized to function in a variety of ways, including to help relieve pain naturally and alleviate the physical symptoms of stress and anxiety. Endorphins work by entering, and in a sense anesthetizing, the specific cell receptors in the brain and central nervous system associated with the physical manifestations of pain or stress. Some endorphins seem to be rather long acting, affecting the central nervous system for hours; others are short lived, lasting for twenty minutes or so before breaking down (Goldstein 1976; Snyder 1977). It may be that past addicts can actually bring about the physical aspects of drug cravings as a result of their conscious consideration of associations between certain cues and their past drug use, working biochemically to activate the related cell receptor sites to particular endorphins. That is, the crave symptoms may result from the person's subjective consideration of opiates and their effects, learned in the countless occasions of using drugs in the past, somehow activating the receptor sites in the lower brain to endorphins that bring about the actual feelings of the "rush" and the consequent nausea felt in the upper gastrointestinal system.

Alternatively, the symptoms of the cravings could be brought about as a direct result of the body's sensing, at the physical level, a stimulus (e.g., the odor of a burned match), which in turn may activate the cell receptor sites to endorphins. In any event, the symptoms must be *interpreted as a craving for drugs* before they can direct or guide behavior toward the use of drugs.

## Overcoming Cravings

Obviously, the craving phenomenon exists. Whether it is manifested to abstaining addicts as a lingering, reinforced memory of the euphoria-producing qualities of opiates or as something associated with withdrawal distress or illness, if abstinence is to be maintained, the cravings must be managed in some way. Successfully abstaining addicts employ a number of social and psychological strategies to lessen the possibility that they will be tempted to renew their drug use and to help them work through and not succumb to any drug

cravings they may experience. Strategies to limit temptations to resume using drugs usually have to do with literal
or symbolic moves away from the drug world; strategies to
manage cravings may involve the use of substitutes and/or a
social and psychological process of supplanting thoughts
about using drugs with other ideas and placing the thoughts
of drug use in a negative context. These strategies are related
to the new identities, social involvements, and related vocabularies that the ex-addicts are developing and pursuing in
lieu of the activities related to the addiction.

In the preceding chapter, I noted that the addict's first
positive step after making a resolution to stop the addictive
use of opiates typically involved a literal or symbolic movement away from the drug world. The effort generally was
made to limit temptations to use drugs again by making it
more difficult to obtain the drug, and to minimize the likelihood of encountering other addicts. Getting away from the
drug, the drug world, and other addicts is not only important
in the early stages of abstinence but also plays a significant
role in helping to sustain efforts to stay nonaddicted. Tables
6 and 7 show how the abstaining respondents reported that
they acted when seeing their old drug-using friends and in
situations where drugs were still being used.[3]

The responses show that even after two years of nonaddic-
tion, most of the study's respondents still elected to avoid
situations where they knew drugs would be used and still
worked to keep some distance between themselves and their
old drug-using friends. One study participant, a 45-year-old
man who had not been addicted for twelve years, still felt so
strongly about avoiding the drug scene that he refused to
meet the researcher at a hotel in Los Angeles because it was
located in an area where he had once obtained and used her-

3. The methods used to manage drug-using situations and in the company of other drug users presented in Tables 6 and 7 are based on a content
analysis of the information provided by the study participants.

**Table 6. Method Used to Manage Situations Where Drugs Are Used**

| Method | N |
|---|---|
| Avoid them | 51 |
| Present self as drug counselor | 2 |
| Not applicable; never had opportunity | 48 |
| Total | 101 |

**Table 7. Method Used with Old Friends Who Are Drug Users**

| Method | N |
|---|---|
| Keep distant from them | 47 |
| Treat them casually | 36 |
| Present self as drug counselor | 4 |
| Converted; give testimonial to God's powers | 2 |
| Other | 4 |
| Not applicable; never encounter them | 8 |
| Total | 101 |

oin. Certainly, strategies designed generally to avoid situations where drugs are used and to avoid encountering drug addicts must effectively minimize temptations to use drugs again and aid in maintaining a resolve to stay free of opiates. Nevertheless, although these strategies may help ex-addicts to remain abstinent, they do not eradicate all temptations to begin drug use again, nor do they effectively manage all cravings for the addictive drug when they arise.

*Managing Cravings through the Occasional Use of Drugs*

Not all of the people in the study were able to avoid using opiates or other drugs, including alcohol, completely after they broke their addictions. Some succumbed to their cravings to use opiates, at least once, usually after approximately a year's abstinence, and among this group were some who discovered that they no longer found the effects pleasurable. A smaller number used opiates (and other drugs) on an occasional, controlled basis. In Lindesmith's, Wikler's, and McAuliffe's views, these people cannot be said to be recovered from their addiction, or cured, since their drug use clearly shows that they still maintain some positive attitudes toward opiate drugs. In fact, sixteen of the people in our study still harbored fears that, under certain circumstances, they might start using again. A common observation made by these respondents was that although they had overcome the physical addiction, they had not as yet been able to transcend the psychological addiction. Table 8 shows the average frequencies of opiate use since the respondents were last addicted.

Certainly, a claim that all these people have truly and completely recovered could be strongly challenged, but the fact remains that, according to the criteria of the study, they voluntarily have not been addicted for at least two years. In addition, most respondents who said that they had occasion to use opiates since the time they were addicted explained that the use resulted from a fortuitous circumstance and that they had not actively sought out the drug. Table 9 shows how the study respondents explained their use of opiates since their addiction. The categories are based on a content analysis of the explanations they provided.

Although all the individuals who had used opiates on an occasional basis might be in danger of readdiction, especially those who reported that they had, from time to time, used the drug in a spree, some of them might not be in serious jeopardy of relapse. They could be in a pattern of once addicted, now controlled use, and they might never become

**Table 8.   Average Frequency of Opiate Use since Last Addiction**

| *Average Frequency of Use* | *N* |
|---|---|
| Never | 63 |
| Less than once a year | 18 |
| 1–2 times a year | 8 |
| 3–4 times a year | 5 |
| 5–6 times a year | 5 |
| 11–12 times a year | 1 |
| 2–3 times a month | 1 |
| Total | 101 |

**Table 9.   Respondent Explanations of the Occasional Use of an Opiate since the Time of Addiction**

| *Reason* | *N* |
|---|---|
| Psychological relief (e.g., relieve depression, tension) | 8 |
| Relief from physical pain (e.g., back injury, menopause, migraines) | 3 |
| Passive social–recreational use (limited to weekends or free days; *does not actively seek* out or purchase drug) | 23 |
| Used in sprees or binges but results from chance opportunity (*does not actively seek drug*) | 4 |
| Not applicable (no opiate use) | 63 |
| Total | 101 |

readdicted (see Zinberg and Harding 1979). In fact, for some people, experiencing the effects of opiates again, after losing one's tolerance to them through months of abstinence, can have an unanticipated and adverse reaction. A 36-year-old woman, who had been addicted to heroin for four years and nonaddicted for almost sixteen years when she was interviewed, described her negative reactions on the only occasion she used heroin after she had broken her addiction:

> It just was so uncomfortable. I came home and laid on the bed and I said, "Never again." It was a drag. It was horrible. I puked. I just went, "I ever liked this?" I couldn't imagine that I had liked it. Now if somebody offered me some, I would say, "No, thank you." I didn't like what it did to me. I didn't like not to be able to see my beautiful children and not to be able to do all the things I wanted to do. I couldn't paint. I couldn't do anything. So heroin holds no attraction for me at this time. (015)

For people who dramatically alter their lives so that they have little, if anything, to do with illicit drugs after breaking their addiction, the effects of opiates that once were pleasurable can come to be defined as undesirable. It is likely that such redefinitions are related to changes in the perspectives of the people involved, so the reuse of the drug, rather than portending an inevitable relapse, may serve to strengthen a resolve not to use drugs in the future.

Some of the respondents turned to other drugs after they severed the bond with the addictive drug. Nonopiate drugs seemed to serve as a substitute for opiates and worked to satisfy cravings for these people. If they were used at all, nonopiate drugs were substituted for the addictive drugs most often in the first year or so following withdrawal. But for some abstainers, the use of other drugs, especially alcohol, continued for longer periods and eventually became a problem in themselves. The illicit drugs used most often were marijuana, hashish, and cocaine; also used was the tranquilizer Valium. Twenty-one of the respondents, more than one-fifth of the total, used alcohol frequently, and in such quantities in the first year or so of abstinence that they reported their drinking had negatively influenced their work and their feelings about themselves.

The use of marijuana as a tool to manage cravings for opiates can be seen in the following dialogue with a 37-year-old man who had stopped using heroin seven years before he was interviewed. He was asked whether he had any cravings during the initial period when he stopped using opiates, and he replied:

Oh yeah. Definitely. Yeah.

*How did you handle them?*

Oh, it was terrible. The desire. [But] I just didn't do it. You know, I didn't. Marijuana saved me. I never used marijuana till that point. Never used it. I think I smoked one or two joints in my life, like when I was on speed.

*So, when you got a craving, you'd—*

Yeah, I'd smoke a lot of grass. I have a very low tolerance of marijuana, so I'd only use a couple of joints when I had to, you know, but it wasn't every day. I just smoked when I needed to smoke it. (074)

Another respondent also claimed that marijuana helped him manage the cravings he felt after he had broken his addiction. This man had been addicted to heroin for two and a half years before he stopped using the drug. The interviewer inquired whether he had used marijuana to ease any drug cravings. He answered:

I used marijuana to ease a lot of cravings, all kinds of cravings, yes. I'm sure that marijuana helped me through it. Because it is a lot easier smoking a joint when I do feel like doing some dope. That helps the time go and it feels better and the thought passes. (085)

Tranquilizers also were used as a substitute for the addictive drug, and of the tranquilizers used in this manner, Valium was the most popular. One woman, who thought she had an "addictive personality," described how she smoked a lot of cigarettes and took Valium when she felt like using heroin. She was asked how she handled drug cravings. She explained:

> I think a lot of what I did was I used replacements like Valium and that's it . . . smoked cigarettes. I smoked a lot of cigarettes. I used Valium, they sort of filled . . . that's what I mean about the addictive personality, you just fill it with something else. Somehow you reach a point where you're not going to go down to that street anymore and nobody is going to come up to you. You've gotten over that time period. If things get really unbearable, I take a Valium. I've just replaced it with Valium. (Group interview)

Using alcohol as a replacement for the opiate drug can be seen readily in a description offered by a 23-year-old woman. When asked whether she ever had any urges to use opiates after she made the decision to stop, she observed:

> Well, I think I might have had urges but they weren't really anything that really got to me. I did drink a lot. I drank hard liquor a lot and then I drank wine a whole lot. I got to the point with drinking that it wasn't a social thing at all. It just got so I would just buy myself some scotch and come home by myself and drink, and I think that was a big replacement. I think it's real common from what I understand. After I quit doing dope I drank heavily for about a year and a half. Something like that. For a long time, over a year. (094)

Another respondent, a 30-year-old woman, described how her drinking problem became so serious after she stopped using heroin that eventually she had to avail herself of Alcoholics Anonymous. She recalled:

I started drinking again, too. You know, I didn't stay totally abstinent, I just went into drinking.

*Did you chip at all—heroin?*

No, that was the last time. I did go back into drinking. I stayed with him and drank for a while. I think I also—no, I didn't even use pills or anything like that. I used pot. We smoked pot a little bit. I got myself into the worst space I had ever been in as far as drinking went. It got to the point where it was uncontrollable, the drinking. And I stayed away from AA for a while, then I moved back out here and my AA contact in New York had been like doing it for me in New York. And then I lost contact with her and got into drinking. So, anyway, and then I got thrown out and I stayed with a neighbor that I had known. She put me up for a while and I went to an AA meeting. I got sober and I stayed sober for seven months and then I got drunk again. I got drunk once and then I got sober again. (056)

At the time this woman was interviewed she was still sober and had been free from her opiate addiction for seven years.

*Social-Psychological Management of Cravings*

The substitution of other drugs for the addictive drug was not the most common method employed by the study respondents in their attempts to manage and overcome cravings for opiates. More often, the recurrent feelings and thoughts about again using addictive drugs were managed by the abstaining person's intentionally placing the thoughts in a negative context and supplanting the unwanted ideas with others (see Mahoney 1974). The physical aspect of the cravings would soon pass, and the person would subjectively and behaviorally be involved in things unrelated to drugs. The extent of this effort can be summarized in a statement made by one respondent, who simply said, "I would think of other things when I felt the craving." This explanation is correct as far as it goes, but it does not convey the true complexity of the process. The management of cravings through the subjective placement of them in a negative context and superseding them with other thoughts is not merely a matter of the "power of positive thinking." Rather, it entails a relatively involved social and psychological process. The manner in which cravings for opiates are successfully "put out of mind" and not pursued is intimately related to the development of the person's new identities, corresponding perspectives, and vocabularies. These new identities and related perspectives provide the basis for defining the cravings in a negative way and the substance for supplanting the thoughts about using drugs.

This social-psychological process of managing and overcoming drug cravings involves subjective, physical, behavioral, and social elements. When a craving arises, regardless of its environmental source, it may be physically experienced as something akin to a low-grade "high" or may be felt as stress or anxiety. Cravings also have a cognitive element, giving the experience both substance and direction; for example, thinking about good-quality heroin, considering the possibility of purchasing the drug, and imagining the effects of using it.

Managing cravings and not submitting to them is accomplished by the people experiencing them by placing the thoughts in a negative context, then intentionally thinking of things that are unrelated to drugs, and then doing non-drug-related things. What people think about, and do, instead of fulfilling the cravings for drugs are intimately associated with the social worlds they are participating in and their related identities and perspectives. For example, some people who have broken their drug addiction become very health conscious and concerned about their physical well-being. When these people experience drug cravings, they may place the thoughts about using drugs in a negative context by thinking about one of the physical illnesses—perhaps hepatitis—that plague illicit addicts. Then they may replace the thoughts about using drugs by imagining the personal benefits that can be gained from some physical activity, such as bicycling. The substance for these alternative thoughts comes from the social world of participatory sports or, perhaps, the special world of bicycling. The abstaining person may then go bicycling, and the feeling aspect of the craving can be masked by the physical exertion or can be interpreted as an indication of exertion.

This is one way in which an instance of drug cravings can be managed and overcome. An effort such as this must be made each time the cravings appear, until the power of various cues to evoke the cravings diminishes and the cravings are redefined as the ex-addict becomes more thoroughly involved in social worlds that are not related to the use of addictive drugs.

It is important to note that the processes of negative contexting and the supplanting of thoughts of reusing addictive drugs are not the same as those involved in psychological "therapies" that attempt to desensitize or decondition people to cues that have come to be associated with drug use, withdrawal distress, or illness. Rather, the processes involve an active reinterpretation of cues and the replacement of them with thoughts that are inextricably related to the identities and perspectives that are emerging and being pursued in the more total life scheme of the person. If a part of the breaking-away process involved a religious conversion, for instance, the ex-addict would be likely to fill his newfound time with a full schedule of activities related to the world of religion. The abstainer's day might involve such activities as Bible study classes, church meetings, providing testimonials to the new faith, prospecting for possible converts, or even helping to repair the church building. Should thoughts about using opiates arise in the course of the day, they would be placed in a negative context—they would be redefined as evil, possibly as temptations of the devil and as tests of one's faith in God. The religious convert would then subjectively and behaviorally supplant the thoughts about using opiates with prayer, and the praying would continue until the cravings passed. In contrast, psychological approaches that merely emphasize deconditioning techniques in treating addicts, although they may include something similar to negative contexting in their practice, typically give little regard to replacing the thoughts with ideas and actions related to the other identities and perspectives of the people involved.

A 32-year-old woman who underwent a religious conversion at the time of her recovery from drug addiction provided an excellent illustration of how drug cravings can be overcome from a religious perspective. She had been addicted to heroin over a seven-year period before conversion to a Pentecostal church three years prior to her interview. A depiction of her as a "gun moll" when she was addicted would not be an exaggeration. At one time, she had been a member of a notorious gang of armed robbers and burglars accused of, among other crimes, the murder of a police inspector. One of the members of the gang was later killed by the police, and some gang members were imprisoned. Somehow, this woman managed to avoid imprisonment, and later she underwent the religious conversion. Asked how she maintained her decision not to use drugs, she explained:

> There has not had to be decision about maintaining, staying off of heroin. There hasn't—it hasn't even been a question. The reason why is because that really wasn't the problem any longer. The decision was, "Do I still want to go to heaven?" The decision is, "Do I still want to serve God?" Do I still want to make sure that my whole make-up and my whole life and my whole being is given to Him just to do with whatever He wants to. That's what the de-

cision is. In making that decision, there is no question about the heroin . . . because God's not going to let me go back on it as long as I stay in His hands. It's Satan's tool, and don't you know that if Satan ever thought that he could get me back on it again, you know. That would be just like—whoever he used to do it. It could be he would have some stranger come up, and one time somebody offered me some—it was in a context, I knew they had never had any before. They had told me, there's no danger of my getting hooked. I said, "I know because you're not even going to like it." It was like they were really so adamant about getting it and I just simply told them, I said, "Look, as far as I'm concerned, you can't even be an associate of mine cause I came from that." To me I could see that. I could see right through that. I could see what it was. It wasn't even like this person was doing that. I could see what it was. (005)

Another respondent, a 29-year-old woman who found God in the process of breaking away from her addiction, described how she would subjectively and behaviorally replace her thoughts of using drugs with prayer:

There were a couple of times when I wanted to fix. I just couldn't. It was just too negative. I mean, I had no choice. I really didn't. You know, something I forgot to mention— probably the biggest factor in quitting—as far as support and everything, was God. You know, prayer.

*How did God figure in it?*

Just in helping me get through that, you know. A lot of prayer, and somehow it seemed to ease the pain in some way.

*Give me an example of how you prayed to God.*

"God, please help me with this." Depending on how I was feeling, the situation where I was. Like maybe I was feeling like I wanted to bash somebody's head in and I was on the verge of total violence. I was shorted out. I was full of resentment and hate and anger and hurt and everything all at the same time. Physically, mentally, and emotionally. Then I'd have to hang onto myself and pray. I was at that point where I just wanted to fix to kill the pain. [I would pray] to give me strength, to take the pain away, to be cool right now. You know, bear it.

*When did you stop making extensive use of God during the whole process?*

Oh, probably about nine months after I stopped using. I'd say the peak of that was probably a year. (034)

Another joined an Eastern religious movement during the time he was breaking away from his addiction. He would fill his time and subjectively remove thoughts about using through Transcendental Meditation. Sometimes he meditated at work, using the same toilet stall in which to meditate that he had used when he injected heroin when he was addicted. In the following dialogue he explains how the practice of Transcendental Meditation was used to manage and overcome the cravings he occasionally felt to use heroin:

*When you first started doing TM, and you were using in the beginning, and when you realized you had stopped, did you have cravings to shoot dope again?*

Yeah!

*How did you deal with them?*

For the most part I meditated; a couple of times I went and fixed.

*You fixed more times after you had been clean for three months?*

Yeah, a lot of things were happening simultaneously, you know, like I was swearing off of it and I got to the point that I knew I was going to stop, but it was a matter which was meditating as much as possible. See, the regular program is to meditate twice a day, fifteen or twenty minutes in the morning, fifteen to twenty minutes in the evening. I was on a special program. I meditated every time I thought about drugs. At work, I would take breaks in the restroom. Go in the restroom and sit there on the commode and go back to my job. Get off from work and I'd go home and meditate. I meditated at least four or five times a day. (045)

Although the *form* of the process used to overcome drug cravings was found to be fundamentally the same among respondents who could recall the experience of cravings, the *substance* varied according to the identities and related perspectives of the individual. For example, those who had become involved in the world of political activists would negatively define ideas about using drugs and supersede them with thoughts and activities related to their new political interests. It was common for these people to define the cravings and the possibility of their succumbing to them as actions that would only provide the "corrupt" state with a justification to imprison them and disrupt the political movement that had gained their favor. At times when they experienced cravings, they would devote even greater efforts to their political work. Similarly, people who had once been athletic and then tried to reestablish that identity when they stopped using opiates would fill their newfound time with various physical fitness activities, especially when they felt cravings and considered using drugs again. The use of drugs would be redefined and now viewed as physically deleterious and incompatible with the health-related identity.

The most frequently mentioned interests that provided the study respondents with the substance to define drug use negatively and replace thoughts of again using drugs were interests related to material and financial things. These con-

cerns were rooted in newly emergent identities and commitments to relationships, possibly involving close friends or
spouses or other family. The negative contexting of thoughts
about reusing drugs and the replacement of these thoughts
with ones related to financial considerations evolved in internal conversations wherein various possibilities were argued out and judged compatible or incompatible with present
concerns and social commitments.[4] One man described this
kind of internal dialogue succinctly:

> I used to think about it [using again], but I'd say, "Man, I
> got the money here. I got a lot of money in my pocket. I
> could go for it, but I ain't gonna have that money for to-
> morrow. And what if I want to buy something for my car,
> buy something, need some money for something? I won't
> have it." (060)

A man engaged in a similar argument with himself weighed
the possibility of using opiates again against other financial
considerations when he experienced drug cravings. Asked
how he handled any cravings he might have had, he replied:

> I have had cravings when I would read about drugs or see
> about them on television. When I would see a documen-
> tary on drugs where it talks about the opium army. That
> was really fascinating. As a result, a craving would occur,
> okay. Given that cravings would occur I would say to my-
> self, "By the time I get out there, pick it [heroin] up and
> come back, it would be too late. I have to be at work in the
> morning." I would rationalize it away. I would compensate
> by maybe smoking some dope. I would say to myself . . .
> and this is real chicken shit, the type of thing that you

---

4. Of course, such dialogues are not always internal; where the abstaining addicts' pasts were known in their current social worlds, the dialogue
often was carried out socially, with significant others who cared for and
wanted to support the abstainers in their resolve to remain free of drugs.

don't tell people. It was eight o'clock. "Now before I go spend fifty dollars," because to this day it takes fifty dollars to get high, you have to spend fifty bucks. It's a lot of money. I said, "Well, you're an intelligent person and drugs don't rule you, right? Right. Therefore, you're going to wait for an hour and in an hour, if you still want to spend fifty dollars, then you go do it." Well, generally if it's in the evening I'd be so tired in that hour that I'd go to sleep. This is maybe a chicken shit approach to it, but . . . I had to do it, the sheer logistics, travel logistics, coupled with financial considerations. (089)

## Summing Up

It is highly unlikely that people who once were addicted to opiates would never be jarred by uninvited memories of their past drug use, even after extended periods of abstinence. Some memories of the addiction are likely to linger for years, and occasionally a latent desire can be awakened by the appearance of a cue that is associated with some aspect of the past drug use. But these cues, and the associations that they bring to mind, can be redefined. Over time, the frequency with which they are noticed, as well as the intensity with which the memory is experienced, can be diminished greatly, if not extinguished.

There seem to be two broad kinds of drug cravings that ex-addicts experience when they are abstinent. One kind results from associations made with withdrawal distress or sickness. These associations may be retained by people who are abstaining and may be experienced as drug cravings when the abstainers are depressed, anxious, or feeling stressed. The second kind of craving emanates from associations made in past instances of using the drug and feeling its effects. Here, the cravings are experienced and interpreted as akin to a low-grade "high." The person feels a "rush" through the body that is followed by feelings of nausea located in the stomach or throat, and he thinks about enhancing the feeling by using the addictive drug. This kind of craving commonly is of short duration, usually lasting fifteen to twenty minutes and rarely longer than one hour. With either kind of craving, the state must be *defined* by the abstaining addicts as a *craving for drugs* before it can have intent and direct or guide behavior to use drugs again.

Drug cravings, which most, but not all, ex-addicts experience, can be managed in two basic ways that can be employed individually or together: drug substitution and a re-thinking about their lives.

As I explained in Chapter 3, to minimize temptations to return to drug use, the initial step in breaking away from the addiction commonly entails a literal or symbolic move away from the drug scene. Such a move does not preclude the possibility that the newly abstaining individual will experience cravings for the addictive drug, nor does the move, in and of itself, help to manage the cravings when they do occur. Sources of temptation and cues that may arouse drug cravings are legion and may be noticed in any environment. Such cues as the smell of a burned match or the odor of urine are impossible to control and may stimulate drug cravings at any time. If they are to recover, abstaining addicts thus must develop one or both basic strategies to overcome temptations and cravings to use opiates.

The first strategy is simply to substitute some other, non-opiate drug when cravings beckon. Marijuana, alcohol, and tranquilizers, especially Valium, seem to be the most popular substitutes. Whether people who replace the opiate drug with another drug really can be thought of as having recovered is, of course, debatable. Nevertheless, although some of the past addicts in our study did develop serious problems with alcohol, most used other, nonopiate drugs only on an occasional basis. Moreover, the fact remains that all the people in the study had not been readdicted for a minimum of two years and the average length of time since the last addiction for the entire group was nearly six years.

The second strategy used to manage cravings for opiates involved a subjective and behavioral process of negative contexting and supplanting. That is, when abstaining individuals experienced drug cravings, they reinterpreted their thoughts about using drugs by placing them in a negative context and supplanted them by thinking and doing other things. This is not just a mental process (e.g., the "power of positive thinking"). Rather, it entails subjective and social elements. The substance for the negative contexting and supplanting of the drug cravings is provided by the new relationships, identities, and corresponding perspectives of the abstaining individuals. If part of making the break from the addiction involved a religious conversion, the abstaining individual might negatively context an emergent drug craving by defining it as a temptation of Satan and supplant the thought with prayer. The praying would continue until the craving passed and the individual became involved in some activity not related to drugs. The person who replaced the drug world with the world of a political activist would replace the craving with redoubled activity in the political movement. And so on. Initially, abstinence is maintained on a day-to-day basis. Each time the abstaining addicts are able to manage and overcome the drug cravings and engage in behavior unrelated to drugs, they are more unlikely to relapse, and abstinence is maintained.

Cravings for addictive drugs apparently happen most often in the first year following withdrawal. After that time, the frequency with which the cravings occur and the intensity with which they are experienced diminish greatly. During the first year of abstinence, as drug cravings subside, ex-addicts also must intentionally avoid the drug scene and other users. At first, they will be uncertain about what they should do with their lives in lieu of the addiction and whether they will be able to remain free of the addictive drug. Once an alternative to the life of addiction is selected and pursued, however, abstaining individuals tend to become immersed in a new social world and intensely focus their activities on a single round of related social relationships. Gradually and increasingly, they become involved in social activities unrelated to drug use. Commitments to new social relationships are developed and corresponding identities emerge, apart from the drug world. These new identities, and their related perspectives and vocabularies, provide the substance with which drug cravings can be managed and overcome.

Each time that addicts can negatively context and supplant thoughts about again using the addictive drug, they can successfully overcome the cravings they experience and continue to remain drug free. Gradually, with the passage of time, as ex-addicts become more extensively and deeply involved in social worlds that are not related to illicit drugs, the various cues associated with drug use are reinterpreted and lose their strength to evoke drug cravings. Finally, they no longer harbor a serious potential for a relapse.

# 5
# Becoming and Being "Ordinary"

When addicts resolve to stop using drugs, they face a series of problems beyond those related to possible temptations and cravings to use drugs again. These additional problems are related to their attempts to fashion new identities and social involvements in worlds that are not associated with the use of opiate drugs. Problems in the construction of alternative identities are variable and flow from both subjective and social considerations. Addicts may be extremely reluctant to engage in relations with conventional people, perhaps out of fear that they will be seen as socially incompetent or that others will not accept them as "ordinary" people. In addition, they may feel shame or guilt about some of their previous actions and shrink from facing others whom they have hurt in the past. Very often, such fears are painfully real.

In the accepted view of society, drug addicts are loathsome people who are not to be trusted and who are unable to stop their drug use because they are sick, weak-willed, and/or immoral. These attitudes are strongly held in some segments of society and create formidable barriers for addicts to overcome if they are to escape from the world of addiction and become involved in a life unrelated to the use of addictive drugs.[1] To change their lives successfully, addicts must fashion new identities, perspectives, and social world involvements wherein the addict identity is excluded or dra-

1. For an analysis of similar problems faced by people who have become chronically ill, see Goffman 1963 and Charmaz 1981.

matically depreciated. At the same time, nonaddicted others must come to accept the abstainers as people who are no longer addicted and act toward them in terms of the new, "ordinary" identities that they are presenting.

The social and subjective transformation of people from the deviant status of addict to that of being ordinary appears for some to happen abruptly and be quite simple; for others, the process is prolonged and very complex. However the transformation takes place, the change involves social and subjective processes that often are very subtle and are not undergone without difficulty. In some instances, the identity transformation results from fortuitous circumstances, for example from an existential crisis and a consequent conversion of some variety. In other instances, the addict intentionally orchestrates the change; there is, for example, a perception of the potential for the addiction to affect the person's more total life scheme negatively and the consequent cessation of drug use. In still other instances, the transformation has the quality of "just happening"; the person drifts away from the addiction and related lifestyle and into a more conventional round of life involvements.

### Courses of Identity Transformation

Substantively, there are three major courses through which the people in our study naturally recovered from their addiction. In each course, the primacy of the addict identity eventually was greatly deemphasized and transformed within the overall arrangement of identities.

The recovery process and identity transformation can occur along a single course or a number of courses at the same time. The course (or courses) taken is a conditional matter and is intimately dependent on the extent to which the addiction and the actions related to it affected, or did not affect, the person's total life and the degree to which the individual had become involved in the world of addiction to the exclusion of other, more conventional activities.

One course of recovery is an *emergent* one. The addicted person, by a fortuitous circumstance or as a result of deliberation and intention, actively attempts to forge an identity (or a number of identities) that had not existed socially or subjectively before or that had existed only in the most rudimentary and socially unrealistic form. A second course, *identity reverting*, involves the reestablishment of an old identity that had not been spoiled by the addiction but had been held in abeyance during it. A third course of recovery entails the *extending of an identity* that existed during the addiction to replace the primacy of the addict identity.

Addicts who are trying to break away from the world of addiction and to put their drug life behind them usually undergo a number of identity changes as they make the attempt. For example, the transformation from a social identity as a drug addict may entail the *emergence* of a new identity (e.g., a convert to an Eastern religion) and the *extension* of an unspoiled identity (e.g., that of a good worker).

Over the course of their lives, drug addicts, like those of us in the conventional world, have been involved in a multitude of social relationships and have developed a variety of identities. Addicts grow older, have children, get married, obtain divorces, develop new interests, and change friends. This is obviously true. Yet the study respondents, when they recounted what occurred when they broke away from their addictions, typically emphasized or focused their accounts on a single identity transformation. For example, they discussed only the change from addict-parent to ordinary-parent and the problems they encountered and solved in that particular transformation. The experiences and events related to other identities—for example, those related to employment—were recalled only as a sort of backdrop to what they considered to be the main transition. This was true even when respondents admitted that the change was "very complex" or "confusing" or that "a lot of things were happening at the same time." Perhaps the study respondents selectively recalled only those experiences that were, in retrospect, the most significant or problematic for them, or only those that were most salient for them given their identities at the time they were interviewed. Whatever the reasons for their selectivity, the analysis I present here takes its lead from the accounts the respondents provided and centers on the primary courses of identity transformation.

Each course of change is conditional. Its success depends, among other factors that I discuss later in this chapter, on the existence and availability of identity materials that are socially and subjectively viewed by the individuals as being compatible with their other identities, perspectives, and values. Identity materials are those features of social settings and relationships (e.g., vocabularies, social roles) that people can use to fashion new identities, reestablish old ones, or extend existing ones. People orient themselves to aspects of their social worlds that seem to reflect their ideas of a positive sense of self. People selectively incorporate these aspects of their social relationships into a coherent arrangement of identities and thereby create a new sense of self. In the case description that appears in the next section, the course of emergent identity change and the problem of the social availability of identity materials are well illustrated.

## Emergent Identities

A woman who had been addicted over a period of three years decided to stop using drugs after undergoing a rock-bottom experience. She and her husband, who was also an addict, were serving time in jail. The woman was released first. As an alternative to returning to the addict world, she turned to her grandmother, whom she had not seen for a long time. Her initial step in breaking away from the addiction consisted of her drawing on a family-related identity that had not been spoiled and a relationship that had not been ruined by her addiction. She did not contact her grandmother to make any arrangements. She simply arrived at the grandmother's house in a small California town with no further intentions or plans in mind. She recalled: "I didn't have any clothes when I went up there. I went there in a pair of hot pants . . . remnants of a fucked-up past." She said she knew that her grandmother would say, "Oh, yeah," and would take her in. She went on to describe what she did when she arrived:

> It was weird; I did nothing. You know what I did? I stayed in the house all the time. I used to write [her husband] every day. He had to go to jail right after me, and I used to write him every single day. I didn't do anything. I didn't hardly even talk or nothing. I just stayed there with my grandmother in the house. I was afraid to go outside because I thought I was going to score. (013)

Gradually, she began leaving the house, accompanying her grandmother to work in the tomato fields on nearby farms. After her husband got out of jail, he, too, moved in with the grandmother. In a short time they moved from the grandmother's house to a farm where he found employment milking cows. At this point, no additional plans had been developed, nor had they formed an orientation to the future. They were in the position of having laid aside one identity and lifestyle without having developed others with which they could feel positive and comfortable. The initial quitting strategy (geographic change) had worked up to this point, but with no further modification and after the initial success of becoming and staying abstinent for a few months, the lack of further progress resulted in confusion and disappointment. In the dialogue that follows, the woman explains both her problem with identity materials and her confusion:

> . . . I remember when we got out there, you know, like you've got to still score. You start thinking about, "Fuck, what are you doing out here with these cows?"

*You had to get to know each other then?*

> We didn't know each other, that's right. It seemed like here we are—finally we're at what we wanted to be doing. We weren't strung out and we find out we don't have a God . . . what do we have? We really don't know each other at all. We could relate all this stuff of the everyday life of being an addict. Now we're in this extreme environment out here with cows and cowshit and in a trailer. This family was first generation from some Swedes. I don't know, I just started thinking we got to bring some spark back into it. We've got to start relating or something. I think we went and scored a couple of times. But it was still different. The scoring wasn't the same. . . . In the past, you go and score and go and interact with all your group of hypes that you have. "Oh, yeah, the stuff is good." Here you just fix and you're in the midst of a bunch of all this country and cows, and it was really weird. It was as if there was something missing even with the high.

*Did you get high?*

> Even that was shitty. I had been clean so long, and I didn't like it. It was weird. I'd liked the high but I was in a different setting, right, and plus being clean all that time. It was just very . . . too different.

The fact that she no longer found the use of heroin to be pleasurable (a key feature of the old identity) demonstrates the distance that had developed between the woman and her addict identity and the change in perspective that had occurred. She found herself experiencing a sort of identity hiatus—having shed one primary identity, not having formed a new one, and not having one in mind that could be pursued in the future. The initial purpose had been accomplished, yet no new purpose had emerged or been adopted.

One fortuitous feature of the new environment she chose was its perceived scarcity of social materials from which she could forge new identities that would be compatible with other existing aspects of the self. The dialogue that follows illuminates this point. She was asked, "Did you make friends up on the farm?" She replied:

Not really.

*Did you get to know the farmer?*

Yeah, but still I felt I couldn't talk to him. I felt like I was on some other planet somewhere where all they had were cows. I changed quite a bit. I hardly ever did anything. It wasn't too healthy but it kept me from fixing. I was like a hermit.

*It gave you time and put you in another place?*

It was like doing time; it was like doing time. (013)

At this point, the respondent's brother-in-law visited the couple, and they discussed their dilemma with him. As a possible solution, he suggested that they enter college and pursue their educations. The woman said that the chance remark by her brother-in-law plus the vagueness of their general situation helped them to decide to go to school and try it out. They moved back to the city where they had previously been addicted and began college. She described this time in their lives as follows:

We started off—we took a bunch of basic courses, you

know. We were full-time students. We joined an organization, a student organization on campus. It was very supportive. We were involved with it. There were people there
who basically—again we were discovering that there were
people there that had gotten into the drug scene, maybe
not so intensely, but they had grown up all around it. They
had seen family die from overdoses of stuff. We were able
to exchange it. Now we're going to school. Now we feel
good. Now we're really going to do something. If we don't,
we're trying—we're kind of advertising that we're making
an effort to do things that are accepted, maybe even by our
parents. You know, I think it was very important, thinking
back now. It's important. We got involved politically with
certain issues that were going on. (013)

Since the time when she broke away from her addiction,
the woman and her husband have had two children and have
continued their college educations. When the interview was
conducted, they were in their junior year of university study,
and neither of them had been addicted for nearly seven years.

This woman and her husband found the new social setting
and the obligations and expectations inherent in it compatible with other aspects of their selves. The new situation
provided identity materials with which they could forge
new, emergent identities and perspectives, and new lives.
Moreover, the setting contained within it people who shared
similar biographies. They were able to form relationships
with people who provided models and cultural support for
their efforts to change their lives. The social materials used
to forge new identities were available within a social world
situated in an existing institution—the university. For other
recovering addicts, institutions such as churches, businesses,
or political action groups can provide the social materials
through which new identities can emerge, be socially confirmed, and thereby help to effect a recovery.

*Reverting to Unspoiled Identities*

As mentioned, the second general course through which an addict identity can be deemphasized and eventually transformed is by reverting to an identity that was not spoiled during the addiction. The process through which addiction and its accompanying problems negatively affect other aspects of an addict's life is neither uniform nor irrevocable. Some addicts exercise discretion and are circumspect in their behavior; with a little luck, they do not ruin all their conventional relationships and thus do not spoil the social identities situated in them. When they resolve to stop using opiates, therefore, they can make their break from the addict world by attempting to reestablish an old relationship and reverting to the identity rooted in it. For other addicts, because of past untoward behavior, reverting to an old relationship may be difficult and may require that bridges to it be mended before the relationship can be resumed. In a sense, old identities that somehow remained reasonably intact can be thought of as having been held in abeyance, as having been "placed on the back burner" during the addiction. Becker (1960) has referred to this situation, metaphorically, as maintaining "a side-bet." When an attempt to break away from the addiction is made, the unspoiled identity is reinstituted, and the relationship wherein it is situated provides the social materials and substance for the transformation.

Reverting to an old but unspoiled identity can be a somewhat easier course than forging a new one. Although the social relationships in which the old identity is rooted may be strained and the addict, thinking about his past behavior, may feel guilty or ashamed, the relationships nevertheless are familiar and can be approached with a bit more confidence than could be mustered with totally new relationships.

The experiences recounted by one man in the study illustrate very well the course of identity reverting. At the time of the interview he was 52 years old and had been addicted over a span of more than twenty-five years. He had grown up and spent most of his life in East Los Angeles. He considered himself an honorable man and was very proud of his street status as a "stand-up dude" who always could be trusted. In the dialogue that follows, he explains how his parents influenced his values. Asked whether his values changed as a result of his addiction, he replied:

Well, my father used to say that a man has to have honor.

*The honor of the word?*

Whatever, if he's broke or anything, he's not worth nothing. That's the way we were raised by my father.

*You believe this?*

Very much, to this day.

*Did you believe this even when you were a* tacato, *a dope fiend?*

Right. To this day, I haven't got a black name or a black mark against me behind my dealings or nothing. When I went out, I went out with true colors.

*You were raised to believe a man's word was sacred?*

Yeah, I believe that. I am my own kind of man.

*What kind of man is that?*

Filled with pride. Whatever you do in life, you have to have pride. That's my way of life and that's what I tell myself. I tell my old lady and everybody. That's the way I believe.

*Did you ever stumble and not do that when you were a dealer and you were hooked?*

I was very well known for that. I always kept my word. For instance, if I told a guy to meet me here at a certain time, a lot of guys would leave them behind for two or three hours. But, it was always on my mind that I had to see that guy at a certain time.

*So, here we have a heroin dealer who when he says he's going to be at a place, he's there, come hell or high water. It's your word and you'll be there. Dope dealing was your only illicit activity, you never did any other crimes?*

Right.

*You had a reputation of this sort?*

Yeah, that's why I can go every place right now with people that are dealing and everything. They don't fear nothing from me.

*They don't feel threatened?*

That's it. I've done it the right way. I didn't run away from those kind of people, my neighborhood especially.

*The reason I am dwelling on this is because there is a lot of stuff written that heroin changes a man's values and attitudes so much that he becomes like a snake.*

I've seen that a lot of times.

*You're saying it's true, but in your case, you're an exception to the rule?*

Yeah, and I am not saying that because I want to paint myself. I am not that kind of man. But, I am proud of myself. I am not sorry for what I did. When I do something, I am not sorry after. I've done it, it's done. But my saying I am sorry is not going to fix a damn thing. (043)

At another point in the interview he explained that he knew that his family was ashamed of him and disappointed in him because of his addiction and because he was a heroin dealer. He claimed that in spite of their feelings, they stood by him through the many years of his addiction. Moreover, he always managed to compartmentalize his life in such a way as to keep his heroin use and dealing activities separate from his family involvements. Asked whether his addiction caused any problems in his family life, he explained:

> I knew they were hurt. It never affected my mother because, whatever I did, my mother was on my side as long as I didn't ask my family for anything. [His father was killed in an automobile accident when he was 14 years old.] I can honestly say that my mother was a great lady because she told me one time, "You're going to learn through this. When you start going to jail and prison, you're going to go alone." (043)

Later, he recalled how his values worked to keep his drug-related activities separate from his family life and thereby prevented the attendant problems of his addiction from spilling over into his family relationships and negatively affecting them.

> I used to stay away from them [his family]. That's another thing about guys like me. In my life, we used to use away from home because I didn't want to get my wife involved. You know, the police would go to your house and bust your old lady or whatever. So, I never involved my family in that.
>
> *You're telling me that you protected your family from your own activity—you kept them separate so they wouldn't get ashamed or whatever?*
>
> Yeah, my life was very different than my life at home. My home was another world. My life in the street was another bag. (043)

In spite of his drug-related behavior, his successful efforts not to overburden his family or hurt them unnecessarily with problems of his addiction, in combination with the continuous support of his family, ultimately allowed him to revert to his family relationships and related family activities when he finally decided to stop using drugs and change his life.

His resolve to change his ways and quit using heroin emerged in the following manner: He was serving a sentence at a federal penitentiary in the state of Washington. This was not a new experience for him. Between 1959 and 1974, on three different occasions he spent time in prison—a total of more than twelve years in prison, in fact—for selling heroin and parole violations. In the discussion that follows, he explains what happened the last time he used heroin and how the drug use and a visit to the prison from his wife effected a resolve to change.

> I've been clean for, going back since 1972, I've been clean. Summer of '72. The first time that I received a visit from my wife [in prison]. I was thinking about quitting because . . . a friend of mine gave me a paper of stuff [heroin]. He told me I'd feel better about my visit. So, I took it and I went in for the visit and I got sick. It hit me right in the pit of my stomach. I had kind of a yellowish look on my face. I fixed it. I was in bad shape. So, it hit me about using stuff, that I was through. She [his wife] stayed [in the area] a week. But, that's when I started thinking, "What am I doing? This is the first time somebody visits me because I am so far away from home, and I fix." That's when I made up my mind that I was through using heroin. It was because my wife is the kind of lady that saves every penny, and she was trying to make it up there. My little girl was born then. She was born when I left, so she was only fourteen or fifteen months old. [And] I was throwing up in the visiting room. Later in the evening, I got my senses back, you know, of what I had done. The fact that my old lady came to visit me after three years of being there. I said, "Where am I going from here?" . . . The sacrifice that she

went through, saving all that money for that long period and catching a plane with the baby for the first time in her life. It was quite a thing.

*She made a lot of sacrifices for you!*

Yeah . . . I started thinking about where I was going. Every time I got busted I was hurting someone that was close to me. Then I started thinking about my old lady and the kids. My wife doesn't work. She is just a housewife. So I started thinking about myself. So, I would have to think first of being drug free for the rest of my life so that I could help my wife and kids. I was kind of thinking about my kids, but I thought about myself first. I had to straighten my life out first so I could help them. I would never go back to using heroin again. (043)

In 1974 he was released from prison and returned to East Los Angeles. He reverted to the various related identities of husband and parent that were situated in the family relationships with his wife, children, and extended kin. They provided the personal and social support for his initial step to break away from his addiction and avoid reverting to the old addict identity and his involvement in the addict world.

Shortly after his release from prison, he obtained employment as a delivery man; later, he became a counselor in a drug-abuse prevention and treatment program that served the same community in which he had been addicted. He developed a strong social commitment to his life, focused largely on his family and his work. He gained a great amount of personal satisfaction from his activities, and they helped him withstand the temptations of the open society (see Becker 1968). When he was interviewed, it had been seven years since he last used heroin and twelve years since he was addicted. In the following passage, he describes his present life situation, future plans, and supportive family relationships:

I've been working since the day I got out. The only thing that is bugging me right now is the housing. That is why I want, I don't know how I am going to do it, to save a little money and put a down payment on a house. I am the pride and joy now. They've [his family] offered to help me if I need it. They've told me if I ever need any help, find myself in a bind, to call them. My son is the same way. "If you ever find yourself up against the wall, don't do anything wrong, come to me." (043)

Identity reverting is not without its problems. And as a course of identity transformation, its success depends on the chances that old relationships can be reestablished. This possibility is contingent on a number of related factors, which vary greatly. Whether an old relationship can be restored depends on the social transgressions committed during the addiction, the amount of hardship and suffering that they brought about, and the extent that others are willing and able to forgive and forget past behavior and accept the offender on new terms. The tolerance of addict behavior exhibited by families, for example, and the ability of some addicts to keep the fact of their addiction relatively secret or to compartmentalize their addiction and keep it and its related behavior separate from other aspects of their lives, works to preserve social alternatives that can be reverted to when the addict forms a resolution to change. If such relationships can be "taken off the back burner" and reestablished, they can provide the social materials necessary to support and confirm a life and identity apart from those formed in the addict world.

## Extending Identities

The third general course of identity transformation found among the ex-addicts in this study consisted of extending an identity that had remained relatively unspoiled during the addiction. The identity extended, although it existed socially during the period of addiction, may not be related to the addiction or the addict world. In an identity transformation, the extended identity is prioritized in the social and subjective arrangement of identities; the addict identity and its related perspectives are either excluded or dramatically deemphasized in the new calculus. This course of transformation typically is taken by people who managed to maintain other identities during the addiction—for example, jazz musicians or bohemian writers—that were not spoiled as knowledge of the addiction became widespread, or by addicts who managed successfully to compartmentalize different aspects of their lives and maintain involvement in social worlds unrelated to the addiction. This course of identity transformation can result from situations in which the person rationally decides to stop using the addictive drug or drifts away from the addiction with little, if any, conscious deliberation or difficulty.

The course of identity extension, wherein an identity that existed during the addiction is maintained and played out at the time when the addiction is given up, can readily be seen in the description given by one of the study respondents. This man was a poet when he was addicted and continued to pursue that vocation after he stopped using drugs. He had spent his early life in the Los Angeles area, growing up in an upper-middle-class family. He first developed an interest in writing when he was 15 years old. The desire to be a writer caused consternation to his father, who wanted and expected the boy to become a scientist. As a young man he was an avid reader and had the wherewithal to travel around the country. At the age of 17, he enrolled at the University of California and attended classes for a time. He never obtained a college degree. He described his friends from that period as being mostly "other dropouts." He identified with the Beat

Generation of the 1950s and early 1960s, and so, when he was 22 years old, he moved to the Lower East Side of New York City to pursue his career as a writer.

He first used heroin when he was 23; within a year, he was physically addicted. He remained addicted over the next four years. He attributed his addiction, in part, to the Beat subculture and in part, in retrospect, to psychological difficulties that he thought the effects of heroin helped mask. He was experiencing problems in establishing his own identity, and he believed that the heroin relieved the anxiety he felt about his sexuality and chosen vocation as a poet. It appears that his addiction was functional. He explained the reasons for his drug usage at the time as follows:

> When I started taking drugs, I had a hard time doing anything I wanted. I had so much anxiety I could hardly move. I felt I wasn't any good and I wasn't sure about my sexuality. Having heroin just took away all the anxiety and all the problems about sex so that I could live with myself. (021)

Later in the interview, he recalled how heroin had a positive function in relation to his writing poetry.

> It was hard to write without being panicked at how poor what I had written was. I had the problem of putting words down on the paper and having them stare at me. But stoned it was a little safer, it was a little more comfortable. (021)

In spite of the anxiety he felt about his sexuality and his writing, he actively pursued sexual relationships and continued to write and to present his poetry. Slowly, as he developed and maintained relationships with a number of women over a period of time and persisted in writing poetry, his anxieties lessened and his confidence grew. He described his growth in self-confidence and his own analysis of its effect as follows:

My feelings threatened me. My sexuality threatened me. My sexual identity frightened me. Over the years when I was taking it [heroin] more, I gradually got used to having feelings and got used to some sexual ambivalence and basically felt just better about myself so that I didn't have to have the drug to feel okay. I knew this in some way. I couldn't have talked about it this way then, but inside I knew that I didn't have the desperate psychological craving on top of that whole syndrome of wanting it physically and wanting the high. I didn't have as desperate a psychological need for it, so that it didn't look quite so attractive to me. Another thing that happened . . . I was able, on heroin, to feel that I could do okay in my career without panicking. It was hard to write without being panicked. . . . I've talked to other artists, it's not such an unusual thing to do. It's part of the process of getting used to putting words down on paper. So several years later I had done quite a bit of writing, but at that point I was a little more into the society of writers and the stuff was about to go public, and that panicked me too. Stoned, I was more comfortable. Then, being part of the drug world, I belonged, so that I could . . . that cuts both ways. I had a lot of hip poems. The feelings were mine. They were what was acceptable in the drug culture and I could write them and they would be recognized by other people as common and okay or, "Yes, I feel that too." So, that gave me confidence. That's having it work both ways. (021)

His growing confidence received further support when, in 1966, he published his first book of poetry. The poems, mostly about drugs—particularly heroin—were written in 1964 and 1965. The work was well received, and he felt he had gained important social recognition from it. The publication of a book represented a sort of symbolic closure on this period of his life, or as he put it:

. . . during 1966 I was needing to put drugs and the Beat Generation behind me; I could understand the things that were not so hot about the Beat Generation at that point. My writing was changing and I no longer needed it for its sake to be part of the drug world. I was getting more used to my feelings and thoughts as I had made contact with people outside the drug world. I was realizing in that year some of the things I had thought before were blind prejudices were accurate observations about people I had been with, the artists I had admired. I had a glimmer that there was somewhere else that I wanted to go. (021)

In the year before he published his first book, as his perspective toward himself and the drug scene was changing, he made a number of attempts to stop using drugs. Each attempt ultimately failed. During this same period, he had two severe hepatitis attacks. He was hospitalized for the second one and placed on a ward alongside a man who was dying of cancer. The experience proved significant in that it worked to strengthen his resolve to stop using drugs and break away from the drug world.

When he was discharged from the hospital, with help from some nonaddict friends he severed his associations with other drug users and left his wife, who was also an addict. He then visited an old friend in Jamaica and stayed there for about a month before returning to New York City.

In 1968 he received a number of invitations to read his poetry in Europe. He accepted, and stayed abroad for six months—gaining further recognition as a poet. After he returned from Europe, he moved to California. He has continued his poetry writing, supplementing his income through various odd jobs, public assistance, and occasional poetry readings and workshops. He has generally been successful in his efforts to avoid reinvolvement in the heroin world; at the time of his interview in 1979, he had used heroin only twice in more than ten years. Both instances of heroin use were in the first year of his abstinence. He described his current endeavors and goals for the future in the following way:

> To keep working at my career. I've written a lot in the last many years and a larger and larger part of it working toward recognition because the manuscripts have been piling up. It will be ten years since someone else published one of my books. I am having a book done this next year. I have done a lot of reading and I've worked up a performance thing with a cellist which is a really nice thing to do and people like and I want to do more promotion for that. I spent the last year writing the book that's coming out this year. Now, I am going to give myself some time to work on recognition and there's another book I would love to have published. It's very short poems. (021)

Some people, then, become addicted but continue to possess other social identities that are not spoiled by behavior related to the addiction or by knowledge of the addiction becoming public. Such social identities as jazz musician and "hip" poet are not necessarily spoiled as a result of drug addiction. In fact, the use of drugs and/or a drug addiction, in certain social worlds, may be sensed as a prerequisite for claiming other identities. Today, for example, this could be true for many drug-abuse treatment counselors.

When another identity socially exists during the addiction, addicts intentionally can decide to stop using the addictive drug and act on the decision or can simply drift away from the addiction by symbolically and behaviorally emphasizing and extending the nonaddict identity in the social relationships where it is situated. These relationships contain the social materials through which the extended identity can find substance and further social confirmation.

**Surmounting the Barriers to Change**

People who manage to disengage themselves from their addiction to opiates, and from the world associated with it, without the aid of any professional help or therapeutic regimen typically encounter a series of problems in the course of their identity transformations. The major problems stem from social relationships, with nonaddicts as well as with addicts. With nonaddicts, the problems revolve around the cultural images of addicts; they are depicted as dissolute, wantonly criminal, or worse. Because "once an addict, always an addict" is such a widely held belief, the pejorative attitudes commonly used to depict addicts continue to be applied to people who have stopped using drugs, even after long periods of time. Addicts, in our culture, are strongly stigmatized, and the social stigma can undermine a resolve to change. Ultimately the stigma attached to drug addiction can turn addicts back to the world of heroin and addiction, where they may feel understood and accepted (see Ray 1961). This, by the way, may be one reason why relatively few addicts manage to get off methadone maintenance. In addition to the addict folklore that depicts methadone as more addictive than heroin (see Chapter 6), methadone programs typically bring addicts together, reinforcing ideas that this is the company in which they belong.

*Relationships with Addicts*

Their relationships with other drug addicts present several problems for people who are attempting to abstain from further drug use. Some of the problems are rather obvious, but others are quite subtle. For example, some drug addicts are supportive of another addict's attempt to stop using drugs, but this is not always so. In fact, it is more typical for addicts to test an abstainer's resolve not to use drugs by tempting him or her with offers of free drugs and/or by strongly cajoling the addict to resume the drug use. Typical of such efforts by addicts are arguments like, "Oh, come on, take one shot for old time's sake" or, "Come on, you won't become addicted again by using just one time."

Other problems presented by drug addicts to the newly abstinent are even more subtle and insidious. These problems stem from the conversation of addicts in which images of drugs and drug use are salient concerns. The poet quoted earlier in this chapter explained this problem in the following way:

> . . . I certainly remembered it the next year when I was trying to stay off and I was finding that I had to keep people away from the door who were in the drug world. I couldn't trust them not to bring it up and I couldn't trust myself around them. I would start slipping into that same mode of thinking, which is pervasive. They complain that junkies just talk about junk. It's not literally true, but substantially it's really true. Their slant on everything is drug oriented, every step along the way. (021)

The temptations to use opiate drugs created by other addicts and the problem of the saliency of thoughts about drugs and drug use, as I have shown, are managed by avoiding addicts and by placing thoughts about using drugs in a negative context and replacing them with thoughts and activities that are unrelated to drugs. The success of both strategies depends on the extent to which the ex-addicts are able to make new affiliations or reestablish old ones with nonaddicts with whom they can feel comfortable and accepted.

## Relationships with Nonaddicts

People who are attempting to break an opiate addiction and put that part of their lives associated with the addict world behind them must find a place in relationships with nonaddicts where they will feel accepted. If they cannot do this, they are far more likely to return to their old ways. Depending on the particular circumstances of the individual, the process of establishing ordinary relationships with nonaddicts can be either difficult or easy. The first step is to overcome the social stigma associated with addiction.

Surmounting the stigma placed on them by the nonaddictive society was accomplished by the study respondents in various ways. For one group of abstaining addicts, the stigma did not present a terribly serious problem because the significant others in their social world were aware of their pasts, accepted them, and believed that the addicts could quit their drug use and change their lives. A second group of abstaining addicts did not believe that nonaddicts would accept them if they were aware of their pasts, so they constructed strategies to conceal the drug aspect of their pasts from their current social relationships. A third group, and these ex-addicts had perhaps the most difficult course, attempted to change the negative beliefs that nonaddictive people held about them and thereby regain the acceptance of the nonaddict world.

Some addicts give up their drug use and, in the course of changing their lives, form new relationships with nonaddicted others who are aware of their pasts. This situation is a typical one for people who are converted to certain religious or political groups. Members of these groups may maintain belief systems that allow them to see people as having changed, even if the group members have full knowledge of the addicts' pasts. Within the group, abstaining addicts feel accepted and can come to believe that they can truly change their lives. Other group members may also share similar biographies. Groups such as these often believe that although people may have behaved in a deviant manner, that does not mean the individuals are deviants—that is, the deviance does not attach to a *kind* of person. Such beliefs, through their ready and open acceptance, help facilitate the identity transformations of people trying to change their world and the social confirmation of a new identity within that world (see Lofland 1969).

Within other groups, however, the stigma associated with drug addiction is thought by the abstaining addicts to be so strongly felt that they systematically hide the fact of their drug use from nonaddicted people in their social relationships. The power of the stigma of addiction was explained by one man in the study who had been addicted for three and a half years. He described how he felt about his relationships with his family when he stopped using:

> . . . they weren't putting on any pressure. It was like they knew what I was and what I did and I'm out and they were glad. To them it was like "everything's right." You know, "If he was bad, he's good now." They would say that to other people, but in their minds, man, they want to think that, but hey, they still got that one thing about you. You know, "You never know, because once he's one, he's always gonna be one." You know that fucking trip. I used to think of myself, "It doesn't make any difference how good I am or what, or what I'm gonna be when I get out again [out of prison]. These people are always going to think—first they thought good of me, but once I fucked up, I was dirt and scum." If I was on the street, man, they'd walk over me. Shit on me. Regardless of how good I was before. You know, if you're an alcoholic, hey, they don't think an alcoholic is as bad as a fucking drug addict because a hype is a person who just drinks socially with everybody and they don't think they have a problem. But, like, anyway, you're marked. And I thought to myself, "You know, people are gonna think the same thing about me for the rest of my life and what I did and what I caused. You know, how many people I hurt." (060)

When the stigma is strongly felt by ex-addicts, and when they believe that public awareness of the past addiction will negatively affect their adjustment to a nonaddictive life, addicts develop strategies to conceal possible damaging biographical information (Goffman 1963). One man in our study described some of the difficulties he had in trying to conceal his past:

> Yeah, it really is a stigma. In fact, in case you're wondering why I'm here tonight, this is the first opportunity I've really had to tell somebody [my story]. What happened, and even then we're not going into all the detail. It's pretty amazing for me at times. I'll be talking to people that I know through work or through other social contacts, they'll start going on about how their brother is a junkie or this or that. Half the time it turns out that they're not a junkie, and it's hard for me to resist arguing with them, and try and express that to somebody without having any, you know, being able to claim any personal expertise. (092)

For other ex-addicts, especially those who are attempting to forge new lives free of opiates while living among people who are aware of the past addiction, working through and overcoming the stigma can be a prolonged and arduous process. Because of the former addict's past behavior and the overwhelmingly negative cultural images concerning addicts and addiction, nonaddicted persons may continue to harbor suspicions about the abstaining addict for long periods of time. These suspicions generally relate to whether the proclamations made by the ex-addict about having changed his or her ways can be taken at face value and trusted. Many people are suspicious of such statements by an ex-addict; they may have heard and accepted such claims before, only to suffer the negative consequences of the abstainer's relapse.

Problems in overcoming the social stigma and related suspicions are further complicated for addicts who desire to change their lives by their own fears that they may not be able to get along with, or be accepted by, nonaddicts. Ex-addicts often feel ashamed or guilty about their past lives, and these feelings may work to intensify their sensitivities to behavioral cues that may indicate that other people do not trust them. Unless they are overcome, such perceptions of distrust, coupled with the problems of adjusting to a conventional style of life, can facilitate a return to the addict community and lifestyle.

To resolve the problems stemming from the stigma of addiction, ex-addicts must prove to nonaddicted people that they are no longer using drugs or addicted. Proof has two interrelated social aspects. First, the abstaining addicts must act in ways that demonstrate to others that they are no longer using drugs. Second, and this aspect also is behavioral, the ex-addicts must demonstrate that they have, in fact, become different persons.

How can this be done? Well, proof might be found in the ex-addicts' maintaining some of the involvements thought of as typical of a conventional, "ordinary" life over an extended period of time. For example, ex-addicts are expected to be steadily employed, to maintain their own places of residence, and to keep reasonably "normal" hours. They should also possess some material things that are common in the nonaddictive world—say, a television set and a stereo. Ex-addicts must avoid, or at least not be seen in, "deviant" places, especially those areas known to be frequented by drug addicts. They should frequent "normal" places—the cinema, restaurants, or sports events—and when they do, they should pay their own way.

These may seem like small concerns, but they are important because they go against the stereotypic images that nonaddicted people have of addicts. For example, addicts are believed to sell their material possessions for money to purchase drugs, or addicts are thought not to spend money on something as "frivolous" as a sporting event when it could be used for drugs. By the addicts' actions and even their possessions, others assess whether their claims that they no longer are using drugs and have changed their lives are true. When these conventional "trappings" are present, nonaddicts are more likely, over time, to accept recovery claims (see Lofland 1969).

The initial suspicion and resistance offered by nonaddicts to a newly abstaining addict's claims to having stopped using drugs and the importance of eventually gaining the acceptance of the wider world were vividly described by a 29-year-old woman in our study. She had been addicted to heroin for five years. Asked, "How many of the people who know you well also are aware that you were once an addict?", she responded:

My mom and my sister know.

*And how have they treated you in this whole situation?*

I'd say better than the average family.

*How did they treat you when you were into it, the dope fiend situation?*

They treated me like I was a dope addict, but they were—well, it's true, you know, they really didn't have a lot of hope for me. And, you know, they never have.

*Were they afraid of you?*

Yeah, I think they were. They were leery of me. They didn't trust me, because of that old, you know, you don't trust them. They were sorry for me. They saw me as something pitiful, because, let's face it, "Once a hype, always a hype."

*You felt they believed that?*

Uh-huh. They were worried.

*Okay, how do they feel about you now? You've put two years behind you. You've come a long way.*

Well, they're killing me with strokes!

*Are they really? They're supportive now. Give me a typical thing your mother does that you call a stroke.*

She'll say, "You have grown up so much in these last two years. I can't believe it! You seem to have it so much more together. It's just fantastic!" And my ego goes puff. And they all do the same thing.

*You feel good when they say this?*

Yeah, and every once in a while, little things will—they'll say, like, well, one of my sisters is real domineering and real defensive and she's the leader type. And every once in a while she'll say something like, "Well, for somebody that started at the bottom of the heap, you're doing pretty good there." (034)

Another respondent, a 26-year-old man, explained what he did to prove to his family that he no longer used heroin:

Well, with my family I had to prove myself. They didn't believe that I was off heroin. Six months after I was off, they finally decided to give me a chance to prove that I was off heroin.

*How did you do that?*

By getting a job, getting an apartment, settling down, not asking them for nothing and watching me. Finally I did. I really felt the need for a crutch then. It was very hard. I didn't know if I could do it at all. But I did; it was a challenge. Which now, I couldn't give a damn what they think about me. Back then I was younger and I was scared and I needed them. The way it is now, they live their life and I live mine. I just don't associate with dopers—a little weed, a little wine, fine, but no chipping, not even a nickel [five dollars worth of heroin]. I wouldn't even, you know, "one more time for old time's sake." I've known too many people that did that and then I look at them six months later and they're the same as they ever were. So, no, I'm not going to do it. I'm not going to take the chance again because this time it would kill me. I know it would.

*What happened to your old junkie friends?*

I don't associate with them. They stopped coming around.

*Did you have trouble making new friends?*

My old friends came back to me. The ones that weren't using stuff came back. They asked if there was anything they could do to help me and if I was out of work or something. I'd say, "Yeah, you could give me a lead to a job or something." They would, and that's how I survived. (017)

It seems then, that the stigma of opiate addiction can be surmounted without the benefit of therapeutic intervention where, for example, the passage through and "graduation" from a treatment program would help confer publicly a new social status—of ex-addict or recovered addict. Surmounting the stigma without such a program can be difficult, but with time, and some persistence, it can be done. People who stop using opiates and who attempt to change their lives can regain the confidence and acceptance of the nonaddicted by acting, on a day-to-day basis, as if they no longer were tied to the drug. At first, abstaining addicts may feel out of place, be highly self-conscious, and have a sense of remoteness from their own actions. But, by being in "normal" places (e.g., going to the movies or dining out), by being employed, and by having the usual material possessions of the conventional culture, the ex-addicts' claims no longer to be addicted will, in time, find acceptance. The stigma of addiction will cease to filter and shape the perceptions and responses of others. As people begin to treat ex-addicts in ordinary ways, the abstainers come to accept themselves as ordinary people and find personal satisfaction in conventional pursuits.

## The Stabilization of Identities, Perspectives, and Relationships

As abstaining individuals remain free from opiate drugs and continue to pursue lives that are oriented toward "ordinary" concerns, a number of subjective changes also occur. These changes are related to the ex-addicts' new social identities and perspectives, and can be recognized in the social commitments that they develop to their new relationships and in the nuances of speech that reflect these changes. These new commitments are revealed in both drug- and non-drug-related experiences and subjectively work to confirm the abstainers' new identities and perspectives. These confirming experiences serve to demonstrate to the ex-addicts the social and psychological distance they have come from their pasts, in both social and personal terms. The commitments also work to form a symbolic wedge between the addicts' present and past identities and perspectives.

### The Emergence of Social Commitments

As the ex-addicts, on a day-to-day basis, continue to manage any drug cravings they may have and avoid using the addictive drug, their nonaddict identities and perspectives are strengthened. Their conventional social world relationships evolve, and their commitments to them deepen.[2] For the ex-addicts, these conventional involvements and pursuits eventually may yield more than ample reasons for not returning to their "sordid" ways. For example, former addicts who marry, have children, enjoy steady employment, and obtain a few material possessions develop important personal stakes

2. The importance of the change in lifestyle for continued abstinence has been noted in other studies; for example, see Goldstein 1976 and Ray 1961.

in a conventional life; they may not wish to jeopardize what they now have by using addictive drugs again. In fact, over time, as they continue to engage in conventional endeavors, the option of returning to the old ways may become less and less a real alternative and more a vague memory.

One respondent described the commitment he had developed to a conventional life after being free of his addiction for four and a half years. He recalled:

> That's when I discovered that whole thing about that one shot. That's all you need once you're hooked. I ain't bull-shitting. Each time you're hooked you get hooked much quicker the next time. If it took you a year the first time, it will take you three weeks the second time. After that, it's an instant high, instant addiction. I know I can't go back. I know damned well I can't. I'll probably be out there forever, man, if I do. It'll take me two or three years to get my shit together. By that time, my kids will be as old as me. By that time they'll be saying, "My old man ain't shit. He's out there on the street corner." I've got so many things to consider and I can't get tied up in myself from this point on. I've got my wife and two kids to think about. There ain't no way in the world I can go back. (054)

Another respondent, a 35-year-old man, made a similar observation:

> I'm in a good space. I'm more positive of who I am and what I am. I feel better than I ever have emotionally. I feel younger in my mind than I ever have in my whole life. But, anyway, emotionally I'm stable in the sense that I want my future to be clear of harmful drugs. I want to do it for my kids, for my wife. I'd like to see my wife quit working soon. (101)

The extent to which the study respondents have been able

to transform their lives and develop stakes in more conventional pursuits can also be seen in the study's aggregate data related to employment patterns, material conditions, and arrest reports. Table 10 shows the kind of employment the respondents held for the longest period, before, during, and after their addiction.

The table shows two major trends: (1) an increase in the number of people employed after the addiction stage, with fewer cases in the "no occupation" category; (2) a movement away from blue-collar occupations and toward white-collar employment, especially clerical and sales positions, after the addiction. Both trends could be taken as indications of an increase in participation in conventional endeavors and lifestyles following the period of addiction. The table also shows that the untreated sample's occupation after addiction has a higher frequency of clerical workers, about the same amount of skilled manual employees, but fewer machine operators and unskilled laborers than the 1980 California census. These figures also reflect a movement toward better-paying and white-collar occupations after addiction.

Study respondents also were asked to assess their present material situations compared with the periods before and during their addiction. Table 11 shows that more than two-thirds (71) of all respondents assessed their present situation as better than it was before and during the addiction. These self-evaluations also clearly show that the great majority of the respondents have moved into more conventional lifestyles, at least in terms of material conditions, since they broke away from their addictions. The latter conclusion gains further support from the data concerning the number of times they were arrested since their last addiction (see Table 12). Study participants were asked in this table about the number of times they had been arrested before they stopped using and the number of arrests since their addiction ended.

**Table 10.  Kinds of Employment Held for the Longest Time Before, During, and After Addiction Compared with 1980 California Census (percentages)**

| Occupation | Before Addiction | During Addiction | After Addiction | California Census 1980[a] |
|---|---|---|---|---|
| High-level executives, proprietors, and major professionals | 2 | 2 | 2 | 18 |
| Managers, proprietors of medium-size businesses, and lesser professionals | 2 | 5 | 4 | 6 |
| Administrators, owners, and minor professionals | 4 | 3 | 6 | 19 |
| Clerical and sales workers, technicians, and owners of small businesses | 26 | 19 | 38 | 13 |
| Skilled manual employees | 7 | 15 | 18 | 16 |
| Machine operators and semiskilled employees | 17 | 11 | 9 | 12 |
| Unskilled employees, laborers | 14 | 10 | 7 | 15 |
| No occupation (e.g., retired, students, public assistance) | 12 | 20 | 4 | 1 |
| Refused to answer; data unavailable | 16 | 15 | 12 | — |
| Total | 100 | 100 | 100 | 100 |

[a]Census includes civilian population 16 years old or older.

**Table 11.   Respondents Assessment of Present Material Situation Compared with the Period Before and During Addiction**

| Respondents' Evaluation | Compared with Before Addiction | Compared with During Addiction |
|---|---|---|
| Worse | 21 | 18 |
| Same | 17 | 12 |
| Better | 63 | 71 |
| Total | 101 | 101 |

**Table 12.   Reported Number of Arrests Before Stopping and After Addiction Ended**

| Number of Arrests | Before Stopping | Since Addiction Ended |
|---|---|---|
| None | 26 | 63 |
| 1 | 6 | 20 |
| 2 or 3 | 13 | 12 |
| 4 or more | 55 | 6 |
| No answer | 1 | — |
| Total | 101 | 101 |

The data in Table 12 show a clear move away from deviant involvements, especially if the data are coupled with the facts on employment and improved material circumstances in Tables 10 and 11. More than half of the respondents said they had been arrested four times or more before they broke away from their addiction, and almost two-thirds of them said they had not been arrested a single time since they stopped using the addictive drug.

*Drug-Related Experiences That Confirm Identity Changes*

The study respondents recalled two kinds of experiences related to drugs that worked socially and subjectively to confirm that they no longer were addicts. One experience entailed the opportunity to use an opiate and the subsequent refusal to do so; the second experience (as I briefly noted in the last chapter) entailed the use of an opiate drug with highly undesirable results. Both experiences served as a benchmark that confirmed to the individuals that they were no longer addicts, because if they were still addicted they would take the opportunity to use the drug again or would still enjoy the effects of the drug when they did use it.

One 52-year-old man, who had used heroin for more than twenty years, described the importance of his refusal of an offer to use heroin. He was asked whether he ever was tempted to use again? He explained:

> No. I'm going to tell you a lesson of that. It's very strong. There's an old friend of mine and he's still doing everything. I got up one Sunday and I was broke. I happened to think of this guy and I called him. I said, "You know what, I'm broke." He said, "Come over, I want to see you anyway." So I go over and I think I got him out of bed. When I got there he said, "How much money do you want?" I said, "If you have a ten so I can get a couple of drinks." He said, "Okay, wait a minute." So he got this stuff [heroin] and I started resting and he fixed. I was standing by the door watching him. When he got through he said, "Go ahead, there it is." I said, "What are you talking about? I don't want it. I just want the ten bucks that I asked for. I'll bring it back later." So I was patient and I waited. I was watching the guy put it away, and we started laughing. So we talked about a half-hour, and I said, "Give me the money, man, I've got to split." He gave me twenty. He said, "You son-of-a-bitch, you're really serious about this." I said, "That's

right, it's all over." He said, "Don't you crave it?" I said, "I don't think so. I don't want it." He started laughing, and he said, "Okay." I went right like that. I've seen guys fix, whatever, but I've never done any. (043)

At the time of the interview, this man had not been addicted for twelve years.

Another drug-related experience, reported by some ex-addicts, which strengthened their resolve and confirmed their developing perspective toward drugs, was to use an opiate again only to find the effects undesirable. A 32-year-old woman described what happened to her when she used heroin after being drug free for three months.

> . . . the time I used heroin after I cleaned up. I'd been clean for about three months, totally clean, caffeine, everything, coffee, tea, sugar. I quit smoking. I got so loaded that I didn't like it at all. I just didn't like it. Rather than complaining like I used to complain, "I'm not high enough." I was complaining, "I'm too high, I don't like this." I was too loaded. I couldn't keep my eyes open. I couldn't do anything. I just sat there on the couch and couldn't do anything. I couldn't talk. I really didn't like it. I didn't like it at all. I didn't do it again. (077)

Surely the likelihood of relapse would be increased if, after having been abstinent, the experience of using again was perceived positively rather than negatively. Negative experiences indicate a change in perspective and help forge a symbolic wedge between the person's new life involvements and the past drug-related perspectives.

*Speech Nuances and Identity Transformation*

As ex-addicts remain free from opiates and continue to pursue conventional rounds of life activities, their identification of themselves as addicts begins to fade into the past. Their new lives can be seen in the nuances of their speech (see Ray 1961). The change in their identities can be noted by the fact that, in time, they begin to talk of their addiction in the past tense. A common observation made by many study respondents was that they felt "funny" talking about their addiction because it "no longer was them." They no longer "felt a part of the scene" because their involvement with the drug world was so long ago and so different from their current lives. The subjective transformation of the ex-addicts in the study could also be noted in their speech patterns, especially in their use of pronouns. As the symbolic and temporal distance between their past involvements and their current conventional lives increased, they spoke of addicts they encountered in their past lives in the third person rather than the first. They now referred to addicts as "them" or "they" rather than "we" or "us." This change might indicate that they no longer strongly identified with drug users. Moreover, these alterations in vocabulary sometimes were coupled with the use of negative adjectives in references to addicts; this further reflected the social and symbolic distance that had developed between the ex-addicts and the addict world. It was common for some study respondents to refer to their past lives, and to other addicts, as "dirty," as being "scum," or in relatively compassionate but distant terms conveying pity or sorrow about the addicts and their world.

A few notable exceptions to the tendency to speak of the addiction in the past tense were found in the study. Some of the respondents still feared that, under certain conditions, they might become readdicted. They still thought of themselves as addicts, although they had not been physically addicted for at least two years. Of the sixteen respondents I mentioned in Chapter 4 who still thought of themselves as addicts, seven had been affiliated with Alcoholics Anonymous or were at some time members of that organization.

These seven former users may have accepted the AA ideology that, in part, supports the belief of "once an addict, always an addict." That is, from the AA perspective, a recovery from alcoholism or drug addiction can be brought about only after people accept that they are alcoholics or addicts, and this self-identification must be retained for abstinence to succeed. Among others who feared they might become readdicted, five were rather shaky in the sense that, although they had terminated their use of opiates, they had not reached the point of symbolic resolution to put that part of their lives behind them (see Jorquez 1983; Tuchfeld 1976, 1981). For example, they still maintained some association with the drug world or had personal problems with other drugs, especially alcohol or Valium. Four of the ex-addicts who still feared the possibility of readdiction seemed stable in their resolve, were in the process of transformation, but still maintained a strong respect (fear) for the addictive drug.

### Summing Up

This chapter showed the courses that people take in their lives when they stop using opiate drugs without the aid of any professional intervention or therapeutic regimen. The manner of termination and the course (or courses) that follow withdrawal from opiates are closely related to the degree that the addicts were involved in the world of addiction, to the exclusion of activities in other, more ordinary worlds, and to the extent that they had ruined conventional social relationships and spoiled the identities situated in them.

The way to an identity transformation hinges, to a considerable extent, on the general lifestyle an addict has maintained, especially the commitments and involvements in conventional aspects of life. The major problems faced by people who have stopped their addictive use of opiate drugs, beyond those associated with the craving phenomenon and its management, spring from the societal stigmatization of addiction. Social stigma presents a formidable barrier that must be overcome if abstaining addicts are successfully to stop using drugs and transform their lives. The difficulties in this transformation may be compounded if the stigma of addiction is coupled with other stigmas (e.g., those associated with race).

In spite of the problems facing people who are attempting to break their addiction to drugs, addicts can and do recover without treatment. They can successfully transform their identities and come to be treated as "ordinary" people. They can do this by *reverting to an old identity* that has not been damaged too badly as a result of the addiction. Or they can *extend an identity* that was present during the addiction and has somehow remained intact. Or they can engage an *emergent* identity that was not present before or during the addiction. A successful transformation of identity requires the availability of identity materials with which the nonaddict identity can be fashioned. Identity materials are those aspects of social settings and relationships (e.g., social roles, vocabularies) that can provide the substance to construct a nonaddict identity and a positive sense of self. In part, the availability of such materials is related to the stigma associated with the addiction.

Those addicts wishing to change their identities may first have to overcome the fear and suspicions of nonaddicts before they will be accepted and responded to in ways that will confirm their new status. Gaining the recognition and acceptance of the nonaddict world often is a long and arduous process. Eventually, acceptance may be gained by the ex-addicts' behaving in conventionally expected ways. Following "normal" pursuits, remaining gainfully employed, meeting social obligations, and possessing some material things will often enable nonaddicts to trust the abstainer and, over time, to accept him and respond to him in "ordinary" ways.

At the same time, the addict's feelings of uncertainty and doubt will lessen as he comes more fully to accept the new, nonaddict life. Ultimately, the self-identity and perspective as an addict can become so deemphasized and distant that cravings for the addictive drug become virtually nonexistent. For all practical purposes, the addict can be said to have recovered.

# 6
## Changing Views, Changing Policy

This study had two purposes. The first was to describe—from the addicts' perspectives—how people addicted to opiate drugs could, through their own resolve and initiative, end their addiction. The second was to analyze the processes that result in a natural recovery from drug addiction. The study represents a modest undertaking, and within its limits, it succeeds. Readers must recognize that the evidence presented here does not warrant the conclusion that none of the participants ever will use opiate drugs again or that none of them will become readdicted. The mere fact that a longitudinal study was not possible, and that study materials consisted of retrospective information with all its attendant problems, precludes stating with certainty whether the cessation of addiction is permanent. Still, it also is clear that the great majority of study respondents have thoroughly and firmly broken their addiction for varying lengths of time—and have changed their lives. They have done so voluntarily, without the benefit of professional intervention or therapeutic regimen.

Like other analyses (e.g., Lindesmith 1968), this one shows that opiate addiction consists of more than a physical drug dependency. It is a multifaceted phenomenon consisting of physical, psychological, and social elements. Some addicts become deeply involved with the drug world and thus have their lives more seriously and negatively affected by it than do others. This variability does not necessarily indicate, as some observers have argued (e.g., Agar 1973; Rosenbaum

1979; Schur 1965), inevitable and uniform stages of deepening involvement with the addictive drug; rather, it may reflect different kinds of involvements with the world of addiction (see Brotman and Freedman 1968; Gerstein 1975; Stimson 1974).

Most studies of opiate addiction are conducted while people are addicted, when they are abstinent in prisons or treatment programs, or shortly after their release from a closed environment. These studies do not have the benefit of examining addiction after it has taken its "natural" course and come to possible termination. As a result, the analyses yielded by these studies often reveal little in terms of the careers or involvements addicts can have with the world of addiction as they mingle in and, possibly, go beyond it.

For a time, some of the people in this study became immersed in the world of addiction to the extent that opiates served as the focus of behavior and identity. These are the stereotypic addicts who have been at the center of both popular and social science thinking. Yet other addicts have gone relatively unnoticed. Some of the people in the study appeared to have been "passing through" the world of addiction; although they may have been hustling and scoring for a time, they did not come to identify themselves exclusively as addicts. Still other addicts maintained an active involvement in the ordinary world, trying to keep the addiction in hand so that it would not spill over and negatively affect their overall lives. Finally, some addicts were neither immersed in the addict world nor actively involved in conventional social worlds. Rather, they maintained a peripheral involvement with the world of addiction while being anchored to it by another person—perhaps an addicted spouse or lover—who was more involved with drugs. For these people, the identity focus was very open, embracing neither the addict world nor any other. Should the person serving as the "anchor" be removed from the relationship (e.g., by imprisonment), the less involved addict may stop using drugs, drift into a more conventional social world, and pursue an emergent identity unrelated to drugs.

Resolutions to stop using opiates among people who have become extensively involved in the world of addiction typically are preceded by rock-bottom experiences or existential crises. Opiate use and the addict lifestyle become intolerable, and a decision to change is made. Reaching a rock-bottom condition or experiencing an existential crisis has been posited by some observers of opiate addiction as a necessary precondition for successful recovery (Bess et al. 1972; Brill 1972; Coleman 1978). Although the findings of this study provide some support for this proposition, they do not do so entirely. Based on the participants' responses, the conclusions of this study follow.

## Study Conclusions

Some addicts who recover without the benefit of professional help or therapeutic regimen undergo traumatic experiences, but others do not. Those who do hit rock bottom or undergo severe crises commonly are people who have become involved in the world of addiction to the exclusion of any active participation in more ordinary social worlds. At the critical juncture, unable to turn to an old relationship in which they can salvage a positive sense of worth, they may develop an *emergent* identity. People who experience these crises are ripe candidates for a radical "conversion" in their lives, and may succeed in overcoming their addiction by becoming members of religious or political groups in which they can find social support and acceptance.

Addicts who continue to participate in conventional social worlds while addicted—juggling the demands of each life— and those who seem to be "passing through" the world of addiction come to a resolution to cease using narcotics and alter their lives under circumstances that are much less traumatic than they are for "hardcore" addicts. The less committed addicts quit when they perceive the continued use of drugs to be incompatible with existing or potential situations emanating from their total life situation. They become "burned out" from dealing with the problems posed by the addiction, or they simply decide that it is potentially too dangerous to continue using drugs. The decision to change is a deliberate one that has a highly rational quality about it. Once the decision to quit is made, these people turn to relationships that have not been ruined by the addiction and extend the ordinary identities situated in them.

Important in understanding the processes through which a successful natural recovery can occur are the problematic situations that may give rise to thoughts of stopping the use of opiates. These situations, especially if they are coupled with some particularly disturbing personal experience, may bring about a fundamental reorientation in frame of reference and perspective. Interests and actions justified as necessary or appropriate when the person was addicted now are viewed as undesirable. This shift reflects a turning against what one was or might become and commences a search for other ways to fulfill one's life. The person who engages in new social relationships, unrelated to drugs and the drug world, may develop new life perspectives and correspondingly find support for them in the course of disengaging himself from the past.

In the course of this research I found two broad categories of drug cravings. One category was associated with withdrawal distress or illness and generally was experienced when the abstaining person was anxious, depressed, or feeling stressed. The second category was related to past instances of using opiates and feeling their effects. This latter form of craving experience was described as analogous to a weak "high."

No matter what the source of the craving experience, whether it was rooted in past learned associations with withdrawal distress or in associations with the euphoric effects of opiates, ex-addicts can and do manage to overcome cravings. Most of the naturally recovered addicts in the study minimized temptations to return to their drug use by making a literal or symbolic move from the drug scene. Although such moves helped ward off temptations, they did not preclude the possibility that the abstaining individual would experience cravings. In some cases, when cravings appeared, they were managed through the use of other drugs, such as alcohol or marijuana. In most instances, however, cravings were managed through a social and psychological process that involved the subjective placement of the thoughts of using drugs again in a negative context and the subsequent replacement of them with cognitions unrelated to drugs.

For example, if part of the process of breaking away from the world of addiction entailed a religious conversion, the abstaining addicts might define any drug cravings as temptations of the devil and replace thoughts about using drugs with prayer or Bible study. The substance for the negative interpretations and the replacement of the thoughts about using drugs were related to the ex-addicts' new identities.

Serious problems for ex-addicts also arise from relationships with other people who are aware of the addiction. Opiate addicts are so stigmatized that "ordinary" people often will not trust or accept them. However, the stigma can be overcome if ex-addicts act in conventional ways over an extended period of time, thus "proving" to nonaddicts that they are no longer addicted. The acceptance of ex-addicts into normal social worlds is essential for the recovery process.

## Policy Implications and Recommendations

Over the past century, American social policy concerning opiate drugs and addiction has undergone a number of dramatic shifts, and each change has had its effect on the lives of addicts. In the late nineteenth and early twentieth centuries opium in various forms was as readily available as alcohol is today. Opium for smoking could be purchased easily, and numerous patent medicines containing opium could be obtained by mail order, at pharmacies, or in grocery stores. Nineteenth-century America, as Brecher (1972) noted, was a "dope fiend's paradise" (p. 3). Opium-based, relatively inexpensive drugs were used by tens of thousands of people, and many of them became physically addicted. Although opium dependence was the focus of some debate at the time (e.g., was it a disease or a vice?), the argument was not a heated one (Kramer 1976). Opiate use was not seen as an outrageous act requiring immediate and strong condemnation. At most, the use of narcotics was viewed as akin to several other minor vices—possibly similar to dancing, smoking, or drinking (Brecher 1972). Opiate users were not subject to the severe moral and legal sanctions that are apparent today.[1]

The public view of opiate drugs and opiate addicts changed radically in the early twentieth century. This alteration in public opinion has dramatically and adversely affected the lives of drug addicts to this day. The passage of the Harrison Narcotic Act in 1914 often is cited as the historical point that marks the shift in public attitude toward opiate use and addiction. Although the act's original intention was to create a new source of revenue and control the movement of drugs, it was later interpreted as an enforcement measure that made the possession of nonprescription opiates illegal. In their

1. My review here of the history of social policy in the United States in relation to opiate addiction is, of necessity, brief. For a more extensive review in this regard, see Musto 1973.

efforts to enforce the law, agents of the Treasury Department managed to close forty-four narcotics-dispensing clinics across the country that had been opened to serve addicts who no longer could obtain the drugs legally. By 1924, it was impossible for addicts legitimately to obtain the drugs they needed (Brecher 1972; Lindesmith 1968). The power of the medical profession to keep the treatment of addicts within its purview was usurped, possession of opiate drugs became illegal, and addiction was henceforth a police matter.

During the same period, the public's moral position on opiate drugs and drug addicts also was transformed dramatically. Opium came to be viewed as an evil drug, the use of which transmogrified otherwise ordinary, law-abiding people into "fiends" who could not control their behavior (Kramer 1976). In spite of the fact that thousands of addicts must have stopped using opiate drugs without the aid of treatment following the passage of the Harrison Act and the closing of the clinics, opium was redefined as a demonic drug that enslaved users in an intractable and unremitting habit.

The ultimate consequences of these events in the history of opium use in the United States are important enough to review briefly here. By the 1920s, the use of opiates involved the users in a criminal career. Persons who chose to continue to use opiate drugs had to obtain them illegally, and a black market in the drugs soon emerged. Selling drugs became an extremely lucrative enterprise, and satisfying a habit became increasingly difficult and expensive. Consequently, addicts, particularly those who were not well off financially, found it necessary to engage in criminal activities in order to purchase the drugs. Addicts, in effect, were forced outside the law.

Remedial approaches to opiate addiction, which gradually came to be defined as personally detrimental and a major social problem, have been debated at least since the turn of the century. The remedial approach typically embraced was based on society's concept of the addict. At times when the addict was believed to be sick or to be an "unfortunate slave" to the drug, then some form of treatment, voluntary or involuntary, was advocated. And because opiate drugs were believed to be so powerfully addicting, the treatment course typically included the removal of the person from the community for at least a few months. Otherwise, it was thought, abstinent addicts would succumb to the power of the drug and obtain and use it secretly while undergoing treatment. At times when the addict was seen as a "fiend," as a criminal who could not control his actions, then punishment (prison) was advanced as the solution.

From the 1920s through the 1960s, a criminal perspective of the addict dominated American social policy. The few public treatment programs that existed during this period— among them the federal hospitals in Lexington, Kentucky, and Fort Worth, Texas—were judged failures (Duvall et al. 1963). Most admissions to these programs were involuntary, and few of those discharged managed to stay abstinent. These facts gave substance to beliefs concerning the addictive powers of opiate drugs and helped promote the myth of "once an addict, always an addict."

During the 1960s, there apparently was an upsurge in the numbers of people experimenting with opiates and becoming addicted to them. American opiate drug policy still was dominated by a social problems perspective, and society responded to the problem in much the same way that it did to concerns involving alcoholism. Opiate addiction was defined as a serious, intransigent problem, a response that was institutionalized in the form of increased control over addictive substances and the voluntary or involuntary treatment of addicts. As the social problems perspective shaped the social policy, it turned research efforts away from developing a more complete understanding of the natural course of addiction through to its possible unaided termination.

Control efforts intensified in the 1960s, with treatment a major part of the society's arsenal to combat addiction. Throughout the 1960s, and much of the 1970s, therapeutic approaches to drug addiction were chaotic and largely experimental. Although there were strong advocates of several forms of treatment, there was no consensus on exactly what to do. Finally, in the late 1970s and early 1980s, largely through the efforts of the federal government, treatment modalities became relatively fixed. Treatment systems stabilized in three major forms: methadone maintenance, therapeutic communities, and drug-free outpatient programs (Jaffe 1983).

How successful has been the American policy of prohibition, including the control and treatment of opiate addiction? It is extremely difficult, if not impossible, to answer this question definitively. As I have pointed out, there never has been a census of the population to determine how many people use opiate drugs and, of that number, how many are addicted. Consequently it cannot be determined, with any degree of certainty, what effect the U.S. drug policy has had on the addict population. What we do know is that the indicators used to estimate the size of the addict population at any one time are unreliable. For example, if the number of hospital emergency room admissions for heroin overdoses drops, does this indicate the effectiveness of police control methods or the successful treatment of more addicts? Or can the drop in admissions be attributed to a change in drug preference? Or to an increase in the number of natural recoveries?

Similar problems exist when we attempt to evaluate the success of a specific policy relating to the treatment of addicts. We cannot know if an addict treatment program is successful unless the rate of treatment recovery can be compared to the rate of recovery that occurs naturally in the population. Even a claim of treatment recovery as high as 50 percent may be no better than what happens without treatment. Yet, no study of this kind has ever been completed. Admittedly, such a project would be difficult to do, but it would not be impossible.

In this context, it is important to note that follow-up research on the posttreatment adjustment of addicts is inconclusive in determining the best treatment modality. For example, Simpson (1983), using information from the National Drug Abuse Reporting Program (DARP), was able to locate and interview 3,898 clients who had been treated in 34 different programs. The clients had participated in one of the three major kinds of treatment programs: methadone maintenance, therapeutic communities, and outpatient drug-free programs. Within these treatment modalities, no significant differences were found in terms of such outcome measures as the use of illicit drugs and the numbers of arrests and incarcerations. Simpson concluded that "the lack of outcome differences between the MM, TC and DF treatment modalities, as well as between the treatment type classifications within these modalities, provides little guidance for identifying significant dimensions of the treatment process. There is considerable variation between treatments, in terms of goals, service procedures, and client expectations, but each treatment appears to be effective in improving outcomes of its clients" (Simpson 1983, 37). Simpson was being very positive in his observations. Perhaps he should have added that "each treatment appears to be effective" *or ineffective.*

Trying to interpret the lack of differences in outcomes between the different modalities, Simpson concluded that length of treatment may be more important than type of treatment. Clients who stay in treatment longer may develop a strong commitment to change their lives and thus may be more willing to go along with any therapeutic approach, whereas program dropouts (failures) may have been in treatment only because of legal or social pressures and may not have developed a firm personal commitment to change. Consequently, they resist the treatment process and leave the program at the earliest opportunity. If this analysis is correct, then the rate of treatment recovery may be no greater than the rate of unaided recovery. In fact, successful treatment may depend on the ability of treatment programs to recruit addicts after they have *naturally* reached that point in their drug careers where they have developed a strong resolve and commitment to give up drugs and alter their lives.[2]

Just as some people decide to use drugs and become addicted, some addicts decide to give them up and do other things. Once addicts voluntarily have resolved to stop using drugs, treatment programs may then be able to help them realize their resolutions to change.

My analysis of the processes of natural recovery is not antithetical to therapeutic intervention. In fact, many aspects of the course of natural recovery—some of which I have pointed out throughout this book—parallel those that are structured into some treatment programs. Correspondingly, treatment programs may be more successful if they will duplicate, where appropriate, the processes of natural recovery that I have described.

The experiences that opiate addicts undergo when they are addicted and during the course of their recovery without treatment suggest several implications concerning therapeutic intervention. First, contrary to existing social policy in the United States, which largely is based on the belief that opiate addiction is a uniform phenomenon, addiction is a

2. This observation gains special significance in the light of Waldorf's 1983 findings, reported in the first chapter. There were no significant differences between untreated and treated groups in a matched-sample, comparative analysis on such variables as background characteristics, reasons for stopping, and coping strategies.

variable condition reflecting different levels of involvement with the world of addiction and different courses of recovery. Existing policy also assumes that all addicts must be treated (voluntarily or forcibly) if they are to break the bond with the addictive drug. The evidence, at least as represented in the data provided by the study respondents, challenges this assumption. Addiction is not necessarily an irrevocable and everlasting affliction. Under present conditions in the United States, people find many reasons to stop their addictive use of drugs and to do so through their own resolve and initiative.

Also contrary to what one might have expected, the ex-addicts who recovered on their own were relatively easy to locate and interview. This suggests that the phenomenon may be more frequent than believed. Yet addicts who recover on their own remain socially invisible. The frequency with which people become addicted to opiates and recover naturally from their addiction goes unnoticed in part because the stigma attached to drug addiction prevents them from revealing this aspect of their lives in their present situations. Because recovered addicts are not available as role models, current addicts do not believe that they can successfully stop using drugs on their own. Since part of the natural recovery process entails the severance of associations with other addicts and the addict world, in order to limit the possible temptations to resume using drugs, current addicts are unaware of the success of those who have stopped using on their own, and typically assume the worst. As a result, a belief in the irrevocability of addiction continues to find support among medical and social science professionals, the lay public, and addicts themselves.

It could be argued that the "once an addict, always an addict" belief has a social function to play. If opiates are thought to be the most powerfully addictive and debilitating drugs, the belief will prevent people from using them illicitly. This simply is not the case; tens of thousands of people have used opiates outside of medically approved settings. It is ironic that the belief, instead of preventing the use of opiates, may work to prevent addicts from resolving to quit their drug use. That is, it may undermine the resolve of addicts to become abstinent and change their lives. It is important, then, that the experiences of addicts who have overcome their addiction on their own somehow be made known to those who remain wedded to the drug. Such knowledge may help convince current addicts that it is possible to leave their addictive drug use behind them.

Although the process of natural recovery shares some conditions with therapeutic programs—especially "family" programs, such as Synanon and Delancy Street, or those that once existed in some California state hospitals, for example in Mendocino and Napa—the process is not exactly the same. Similarities between the processes of treated and natural recovery include the following: (1) an attempt to destroy existing identities rooted in the drug world; (2) the common structuring of exclusionary group membership during the initial stage of abstinence, even if it means breaking up couples; (3) the establishment of social networks to support the new identities, corresponding perspectives, and vocabularies that are being shaped and developed in the program in lieu of those related to the addict world; and (4) the provision of some social-psychological techniques that can be used to neutralize drug cravings when they appear (see Hawkins and Wacker 1983; Volkman and Cressey 1963).

Although parallels exist between treatment programs and natural recovery, most drug rehabilitation programs, like the existing social policy, treat addicts as if they are all alike. The programs are designed to treat stereotypic addicts, those immersed in the world of addiction that provides the primary focus of their identities. For example, part of the treatment strategy is to destroy the addict identity through a process of symbolic mortification while attempting to develop ordinary identities that can become a new source of motivation. But all addicts are not alike. Whether mortification should be a necessary condition of the recovery process should be determined by exploring for the existence of conventional social relationships and identities to which the person can turn in place of the addiction. If such relationships exist, resocialization may not be imperative. Intervention may simply take the form of helping those who desire to stop using drugs to establish or mend bridges to social relationships in which conventional identities can be played out. In instances where people, as a result of the addiction, have irrevocably destroyed past personal relationships, alternatives that can facilitate the recovery process may be found within existing social institutions, such as universities, churches, and political groups.

Addicts also differ in terms of geographic location, ethnicity, and gender. Drug users in New York City may be very different from those in Miami, Chicago, or San Francisco. In fact, drug users and addicts may differ considerably in various locations within the same city (see Agar and Feldman 1980).

Similarly, treatment approaches that are effective with some ethnic groups may be total disasters with others. If the analysis I present here is correct, in that natural recovery from addiction depends, in part, on the availability of social roles and corresponding identities that can be assumed instead of those related to the addiction, then some groups will experience more difficulties in recovering than will others. Social roles and the identities that go with them are not distributed equally in society. Racial prejudices, class and sexual discrimination, and social stigma still shape the opportunities of people in American society. For example, a white, middle-class, high-school-educated, male addict will have more personal and social resources to draw from when he decides to give up drugs than will a Chicano addict living in a barrio. In fact, a relatively uneducated Chicano addict may opt to retain the junkie–dealer role and identity because it provides him with greater status and financial rewards than any other social role available to him.

Women addicts face similar problems in the recovery process. In addition to the general problems that arise from sexual discrimination, the stigma connected with addiction is probably greater for women than for men. The social image of the "fallen woman" is much more severe and devastating than that of the wayward man. Consequently, family and friends may be much less willing to accept a woman ex-addict than they would a man ex-addict (see *Proceedings of the Institute* 1973). Moreover, women often face different problems from men in their recoveries, some of them revolving around the custody of minor children. Although treatment programs specializing in the care of women are now emerging, most programs still are dominated by men and oriented to deal with male addicts (see Rosenbaum 1979). Yet variations in treatment programs must be considered in any approach, for they will play an important part in the success of the recovery process.

As I noted earlier, beyond helping those who are inclined to give up their use of opiates to make the initial contacts with conventional others, some aid might be provided to relieve the fears and suspicions of nonaddicts that flow from the stigma of addiction, especially in the first year or so of dealing with the abstainer. These suspicions, although unfortunately often well founded, can nevertheless work to undermine the resolve of addicts to change their lives. The negative impact of such fears could be minimized through group discussions with family members, friends, or employers.

In conjunction with the foregoing recommendations, it would be beneficial if some advice could be extended to abstaining addicts that would help them manage the cravings for drugs they may experience. Guidance in managing cravings might be offered to abstaining addicts in the form of teaching them biofeedback techniques or Transcendental Meditation, or by pointing out to them the possible utilization of physical exercise or prayer. It is important to remember, however, that if these techniques are to succeed, the negative contexting and subjective replacement of the ideas about using drugs again should be done in a way that is at least compatible with the existing or emerging identities of the addicts that are not related to the addict world. The mere utilization of, for example, deconditioning techniques may not be sufficient to manage and overcome drug cravings if the techniques are not given social substance in the actual lives of the addicts.

Because it helps to negate craving experiences, methadone may also be useful in facilitating recovery for some addicts, particularly in the early stages of cessation. Nevertheless, there is a common belief among addicts that methadone is even more strongly addictive than heroin (Hunt et al., n.d.). This belief may prevent many addicts from seeking methadone maintenance as an alternative to their opiate use and may stop them from trying to get off methadone once they have started on it. As was true for those addicts who recovered from opiate addiction on their own, those who managed to stop using methadone also become virtually invisible. They are not seen "on the streets" or in methadone clinics. Thus, neither clinic staff members nor addicts who remain on methadone know that some people have successfully gotten off methadone and have not died, gone to prison, or become readdicted. If methadone is to be used to facilitate the recovery process, the addict folklore concerning the unusual power of its addiction must be shattered. Also, it seems that methadone maintenance should be used only in conjunction with a "natural" or formal program that emphasizes the separation from other addicts and the development of relationships and identities that are independent of those related to addiction.

Obviously, as is common with most research endeavors, this work raises a series of additional research questions. As

I have noted, the study was modest in that it was done in retrospect among a relatively small sample of people located through a chain-referral method. The work represents only a beginning in understanding the natural recovery process, a process that I believe is important enough to warrant further research.

All the data used in the analysis were gathered subsequent to the events in question. The use of retrospective materials, although it has certain advantages, also has drawbacks. Problems stem from the vulnerability of human memory, including the inevitable reconstruction of past events on the basis of new experiences and vocabulary. Consequently, I recommend that longitudinal studies be conducted of addicts as they actually move through to a course of natural recovery. These should be ethnographic studies done "up close" that focus on the problems addicts face when they attempt to abstain and how these problems are or are not overcome.[3] Especially important here would be observations of how the various reactions of nonaddicts either facilitate or stymie the recovery process.

Finally, a comparative analysis of the processes of natural recovery, sometimes called spontaneous remission, in other substantive areas of addictive behavior—perhaps alcoholism, obesity, or cigarette smoking—would broaden our understanding of addiction and possibly result in the formulation of a formal theory of addiction and natural recovery from addiction.[4] Studies such as these could be used to fabricate more sensitive and, perhaps, more effective therapeutic regimens for those people who wish to avail themselves of treatment.

3. For a fuller discussion of ethnographic research and its relation to social policy, see Akins and Beschner 1980.
4. An initial attempt to create such a theory can be found in Stall and Biernacki 1986.

APPENDIXES   REFERENCES   INDEX

# Appendix A. Methods and Techniques

The idea for this research originated several years ago during a study I was conducting of people who had stopped smoking marijuana (Biernacki and Davis 1970). Although the reasons some people gave for finding it necessary to stop using marijuana might today seem insignificant, it was of interest at that time. Regardless of the relative importance of the research, it did bring me into contact with people who had been addicted to opiates along with marijuana, and who had stopped using the opiate drugs. This chance discovery of a few "naturally" recovered addicts opened the door to a slew of questions about the ultimate fate of opiate addicts. Were the cases I found unusual? Were most addicts destined to remain addicted for their entire lives? Was some form of therapeutic intervention always necessary to break an opiate addiction? Or was it possible, at least for some people, to break the addiction and recover through their own resolve and effort?

After due consideration, I concluded that the phenomenon of natural recovery from opiate addiction warranted further inquiry. Over the next few years, I continued to maintain my interest and was able to study several more recovered addicts as I became aware of them. During the same period, I applied to a number of institutes for financial support for a project to study the natural process of de-addiction, but I was without luck. Then, in mid-1978, inquiry began in earnest when I (along with Dan Waldorf) received support from the National Institute on Drug Abuse to conduct a study for two years.

**Chain-Referral Sampling**

The research plan was to locate naturally recovered addicts for study by employing the chain-referral sampling method.[1] Chain-referral, or snowball, sampling is a method that has been used widely in qualitative sociological research. The method yields a study sample through referrals made by people who share, or know of others who possess, some characteristic that is of research interest. The method is well suited to a number of research purposes and is particularly applicable when the focus of study is on a sensitive issue, possibly one concerning a relatively private matter and thus requiring the knowledge of insiders to locate people for the study. In dealing with deviant behavior, especially research on drug use and addiction, snowball sampling has been used to gather materials for studies now thought to be classics in the field. It was used in Lindesmith's original study of opiate addiction (1968) as well as in Becker's work on marijuana smokers (1963).

In spite of the widespread use of chain-referral sampling in qualitative sociological research, little has been written specifically about the method. The little existing methodological literature on the subject has suggested that the chain-referral method is a self-contained and self-propelled phenomenon, in that once started, it somehow proceeds magically on its own. Our study showed that this simply was not the case. Rather, the project staff discovered that the sample's

1. Much of the material presented in this appendix appears in a somewhat different form in an article co-authored with Dan Waldorf (Biernacki and Waldorf 1981). That article was published in *Sociological Methods and Research* 10, 1981, pp. 141–163. © by Sage Publications and used with permission.

In still another version, the materials formed the basis of a presentation I gave at the annual meeting of the American Sociological Association, Boston, 1979.

initiation, progress, and termination had to be actively and deliberately developed and controlled. In addition, a number of other methodological problems arose with the use of the method. The discussion that follows focuses on those methodological problem areas; analytically they are distinct but procedurally interrelated when utilizing the chain-referral sampling method. Specific problem areas are as follows:

- Finding respondents and starting referral chains
- Verifying the eligibility of respondents
- Engaging respondents as research assistants
- Controlling the kinds and numbers of cases in a chain
- Pacing and monitoring chains and data quality

## Starting Referral Chains

The first problem the staff confronted when using the chain-referral method to locate a study sample was the social visibility of the target population. Many possible study populations—for example, police, nurses, or schoolteachers—have a relatively high social visibility. A researcher may have some difficulty obtaining access to these populations, but knowledge of where to locate them is not a problem. Because of moral, legal, and/or social sensitivities surrounding their behavior, other possible study populations have a very low visibility and as a result pose serious problems for the researcher wishing to locate and contact potential respondents. This is true, for example, if one wishes to study arsonists who are not in institutions, women who have undergone abortions, or, as in this study, ex-heroin addicts, particularly those who have never been in treatment (see Becker 1970; Henslin 1972).

The ideal method of locating people who maintain a low visibility because of past or current histories of deviance is to draw a representative sample of all adults in the population. Then, having drawn the sample and assuming the honesty of the respondents, you screen the people in it to locate and interview recovered addicts. This method was excluded, in part, because the costs involved in drawing a large enough sample to locate a hundred untreated ex-addicts would have been prohibitive.[2] In addition, the goal of the research was not to test a series of predetermined hypotheses on a representative sample that would allow for extrapolation to a larger population. Instead, the goal was to explore and analyze, in the manner suggested by Glaser and Strauss (1967), the social and psychological processes that worked to bring about a self-initiated cessation from opiate addiction.

Locating and interviewing ex-addicts who had undergone some form of treatment would have presented few difficulties. These people could be located easily with the formal and informal assistance of various treatment program directors and staff personnel who knew individuals who met the research criteria and could refer them to the project. Ferreting out respondents who met the research criteria for *natural recovery* was another matter. Obviously, drawing a probability sample was impossible with such a group, since the characteristics of this population were not known. In fact, because of the widely held belief that "once an addict, always an addict," many clinicians and researchers in the field thought that naturally recovered addicts, the focus of the proposed study, did not exist, or if they did, it was not with any great frequency. That is, the prevailing image of heroin addiction generally holds that the behavior pattern is so powerfully reinforcing that it is virtually impossible for a person to break the tie to the drug successfully without some form of therapeutic assistance.

Originally it was expected that treated ex-addicts would

2. For example, O'Donnell and his colleagues (1976) found, in a sample of all males in the United States born between 1944 and 1954 who were known to their draft boards ($N = 2,510$), that only 2 percent of the cases could possibly be thought of as having been opiate addicted (heavy users were defined as those having used heroin more than a hundred times).

provide referrals to untreated ex-addicts. Except in a few instances, this did not occur. In fact, many treated ex-addicts, particularly those who had been in therapeutic communities (e.g., Synanon), shared the conventional belief and were skeptical about the possibility that addicts could recover without treatment. This skepticism probably was rooted in their own past experiences of repeated relapses following voluntary attempts at abstinence and the testimonial that their current drug-free state was the result of successful treatment. The skepticism might also reflect the fact, discovered in the course of the research, that naturally recovered addicts are much less socially visible and more isolated from other ex-addicts than are those who had been in a treatment program. Although the research revealed a few exceptions to this finding—for example, a small number of untreated ex-addicts were found in larger organizations, such as religious or political groups—they were relatively infrequent. Moreover, the basis for membership in these groups was not the common experience of past addiction (as it was with ex-addicts who had been treated), but a common religious or ideological experience. In any event, treated ex-addicts rarely, if ever, know of people who are successful in their personal attempts to break an addiction and are thus skeptical about this possibility.

Finding untreated ex-heroin addicts and starting referral chains among them in part was accomplished in a manner similar to that used when testing hypotheses deduced from existing theory or areas of knowledge. When the research aim is to test existing theory, the theory clearly and specifically identifies the relevant study population. Although the intent of the research was not exclusively to test theory, the relevant available knowledge concerning recovery from opiate addiction was used, whenever possible, to determine where data outcroppings (Webb et al. 1966) might exist, and referral chains were initiated. For instance, several available studies do suggest that some addicts recover from their addiction without treatment (for a review of this literature, see Waldorf and Biernacki 1979), and although these studies offered little in the way of substantive analysis of the processes involved, they were initially helpful in pointing out possible data sources. One source of direction was provided by Lee Robins's study of Vietnam war veterans (1973). Her research showed that very few of the veterans who had become addicted in Vietnam were still using narcotics three years after they returned to the United States, and an even smaller number had been in treatment. This suggested that one possible source for locating naturally recovered addicts would be contacts that could be developed among groups of Vietnam veterans.

Other studies suggested additional data sources. For example, it is widely known that some ex-addicts, although they no longer use opiates or use them only on occasion, develop serious problems with alcohol. This information indicated that respondents might be found among such groups as Alcoholics Anonymous and in various urban missions—a theory that proved correct. A number of contacts and referral chains were successfully developed with people who had become heavy users of alcohol following their recovery from drug addiction.

Still other studies had shown that because of the lifestyle associated with the use of heroin, heroin addicts frequently committed crimes and were imprisoned. This suggested that ex-addicts might be found among groups of ex-felons. And, indeed, a number of naturally recovered addicts were found in prison reform groups and special university programs for ex-offenders.[3]

3. This procedure is similar to the theoretical sampling procedures discussed by Glaser and Strauss (1967), but the direct intent here is to find possible sources of data; only indirectly is the aim to explore and develop emerging concepts and processes.

Occasionally, contacts and referral chains were initiated somewhat fortuitously. It was not entirely a process of chance, but resulted from an increased sensitivity and attentiveness to information related to the study's focus that developed as staff members became steeped in the research area. In a sense, the prepared mind both knows and can take maximum advantage of opportunity. Thus a number of fortuitous contacts were made; a few, but not all, of them sprung a series of additional referrals and interviews. For example, some respondents were located through the news media, and four interviews were obtained as a result of one of the project staff's participation in a poetry workshop. In this instance, a guest poet read one of his works that dealt with his past experiences as a heroin addict. The poet was told about the study and agreed to be interviewed; he, in turn, made referrals to three more respondents. Three of the four individuals had known each other while they were addicted some years ago in New York's Greenwich Village.

Once the original contacts used to start chains were exhausted, project staff members were faced with the problem of initiating new ones. When we moved into areas where we had few or no preestablished contacts, new difficulties arose, for we had little reason to trust or accept at face value the respondents referred to the project. In addition, some areas that theoretically were expected to yield a high number of respondents turned out to be false starts or yielded too few respondents relative to the effort required to gain access in order to initiate new chains. For example, at one point in the study successful efforts to locate ex-addicts in a Pentecostal church directed the sampling effort to the Black Muslims, where it was thought other converted ex-addicts would be found. After spending a number of weeks establishing the project's legitimacy, however, only one respondent was located in a mosque.

Verification of respondent eligibility as well as the accounts provided by respondents became increasingly problematic as the sources used to initiate referral chains became more distant and knowledge about the sources less personal. One problem here was related to training de facto research assistants. In this study, once the original contacts were exhausted, the sampling effort was theoretically directed to different groups (e.g., Pentecostal churches, women's political organizations, and various ex-offender programs on university campuses) in which new chains might be started. Engaging program or organizational personnel to assist in the effort required, first, that certain ethical issues concerning confidentiality be resolved and, second, that the new personnel be trained to find, screen, and refer possible qualified respondents to the project. Ethical concerns prevented the members from directly contacting many potential respondents; consequently, program directors or personnel who knew of possible respondents were requested to make the initial contact and then ask those who were willing to cooperate to contact the project personally. In each instance the newly recruited research assistants had to be trained to understand and accept the eligibility criteria of the research. This task often was difficult because it violated some common-sense understandings concerning treatment and nontreatment. For example, many people defined themselves as "untreated" in spite of long stays in civil commitment programs because their sojourns in these institutions were involuntary and/or because they had become readdicted on their release and then recovered at a later time.

Similar problems emerged as word about the project spread among friends and colleagues, who provided an occasional referral. Sometimes these referrals also turned out to be false starts. For example, several referrals made by friends of the research staff who thought that their contacts were untreated ex-addicts were, on the contrary, people who had been treated for their addiction. These false starts often resulted from negative or relatively limited experiences with treatment. That is, many recovered addicts have received some form of treatment but do not in any way attribute their cessation of opiate use to the experience; such repudiations of treatment were taken by other people as meaning that no treatment was involved.

In still other instances, the project staff found it advantageous to canvass and possibly stimulate new chains through letters sent under the auspices of a program believed to contain a good potential for revealing respondents. Near the end of the project (in the nineteenth month), we also found it necessary to advertise for respondents. The following ad was placed in local, major, and "underground" newspapers:

> *Ex-opiate addicts wanted for interviews;*
> *will pay, call collect* [telephone numbers].

The "pay" referred to a twenty-dollar honorarium given to each person who participated in the study. People who responded to the notice were screened over the telephone and an interview appointment was made with those who met the major research criteria. The interview was scheduled for a week or two in the future. Although this method for locating respondents worked reasonably well, we decided that these kinds of strategies should be employed only as a last resort and, when used, that special care should be given not to reveal all the criteria of eligibility for the study nor too few criteria. Revealing too many eligibility criteria would result in problems related to verification, while revealing too few details would create management problems related to screening and perhaps difficulties in turning away ineligible but willing study participants. Certainly, in terms of the veracity of study findings and in spite of the management problems it might pose, the latter course would be the more desirable.

**Verifying the Eligibility of Respondents**

In many areas of research, self-presentations made by voluntary respondents cannot be taken at face value (see Douglas 1976). This proscription was particularly evident in our study because of the focus of the inquiry and as a result of the twenty-dollar honorarium given to each participant. (Twenty dollars seemed to us a small amount of money, but unexpectedly it proved enticing enough for a few people to attempt a ruse and pose as ex-addicts.) It could not be assumed that the people who presented themselves as ex-addicts had even been addicted or, if addicted, had recovered. Staff members were forced to take a distrustful stance toward potential respondents, and the accounts that they provided were verified through independent sources.

Verification of the respondents' accounts generally was accomplished through third parties—the data sources were triangulated (see Denzin 1970; Webb et al. 1966). People who knew the respondents personally were asked to validate such critical aspects of their stories as the fact of their recovery and the length of addiction. In many instances, third-party verification was accomplished through the person (a locator) who had started a snowball by contacting respondents who were personally known by him or her to fit the research criteria.

Although independent verification of the accounts was possible for most respondents, in a few instances members of the staff were suspicious of the claims made by the ex-addicts. Suspicions were grounded in discrepancies that the interviewer noted in a respondent's story, in a respondent's becoming unusually agitated during an interview (which might have indicated the possible onset of withdrawal symptoms), or in situations where a potential respondent (or a number of them) came into the project office requesting to be interviewed without having been referred to us by someone we knew. Several strategies, some planned and others that evolved in the course of the research, were used to temper suspicions concerning the veracity of the accounts given by certain respondents. These strategies, although they were not definitive tests of validity, were nevertheless especially crucial in helping to confirm (indirectly) that the respondent was not currently addicted.

Urinalysis was considered as a possible method of verifying opiate abstinence, but we rejected it for two reasons. First, it is known that some addicts will go to extraordinary lengths to present themselves as drug free. For example, addicts have been known to substitute the urine of a nonaddicted person in order to pass a monitoring or surveillance system. Direct observation would have been required to ensure the validity of the urine, and this was felt to be demeaning to both the potential respondent and the research staff. In addition, even if urinalysis had been used, it would not have shown how long a respondent had or had not used opiate drugs. Also, an a priori decision to exclude from the study potential respondents whose urinalysis proved positive might have omitted from the research a possibly important variation of the recovery process—people who are no longer addicted but who continue to use heroin on occasion in a controlled manner (see Zinberg and Jacobson 1976).

One strategy used to corroborate the veracity of a respondent's presentation was made possible through a feature of the chain-referral method. By definition, a chain-referral sample is created through a series of referrals made within a circle of people who know one another. Members of the research staff regularly interviewed people who were mutual friends and/or relatives. Often, respondents would discuss not only their own experiences but those of others, and this volunteered information was used as an additional source of verification in related cases.

The interviewers also might ask to examine a respondent's

arms in order to check for relatively fresh signs of needle injections. It was assumed that an individual who was currently addicted would not go to the trouble of injecting narcotics in other body areas and allowing the arms to heal in order to give the impression of not using drugs just to collect the twenty-dollar honorarium.

A general screening policy was developed after two different referral chains turned into avalanches, and the project office was deluged with unvouched-for people demanding to be interviewed. The policy was not to interview any unsolicited walk-ins immediately, but to screen them; if they were found to meet the research criteria, separate interview appointments were made for them at least a week in the future. This policy was enacted particularly in those instances when several people arrived at the office together, without referral or appointment. The assumption here was that the relatively chaotic life associated with opiate addiction would make it highly unlikely that a currently addicted person would schedule and be able to keep an appointment made a week or two in the future.

Other means to verify cases indirectly also emerged and were utilized in the course of the research. One ex-felon who had become associated with the project staff had the opportunity to observe two study respondents refuse an offer to use heroin while he was visiting a friend in a downtown fringe-area hotel. A field report was made for the respondents in question, as was done for other respondents when relevant information about them reached the project. In two instances, information shared with the research staff suggested that two respondents had suffered a relapse and were readdicted. Field reports were made, and the respondents were removed from the successfully recovered sample until the information could be substantiated. When the readdiction was confirmed (one called the project and admitted being readdicted, and the other was observed using heroin), these respondents were permanently removed from the sample and used for comparative analysis.

## Engaging Respondents as Research Assistants

Finding possible data outcroppings on the basis of existing and emerging theory and knowledge restricted the initiation of referral chains to those areas in which the staff members had some knowledge and fairly easy access. From time to time, it was fruitful to use both paid and unpaid persons to help locate new respondents and start new referral chains. These locators served two interrelated purposes: (1) Because of their pasts, occupations, social positions, and/or lifestyles, they had better access to certain data sources and could more efficiently make contacts for possible interviews; and (2) because the locators often knew the persons they referred to the study, they could verify the respondent's accounts.

The use of locators in snowball sampling is akin to the use of significant informants in field studies. The employment of these individuals assumes that knowledge is distributed differentially and that certain persons, as a result of their past or present situations, have greater accessibility to and knowledge about a specific area of life than others do. These persons can more easily develop referral chains because they may already be aware of potential respondents or may be likely to have others reveal their potential to them.

One excellent locator in our study was an ex-addict and ex-felon whose current lifestyle revolved around certain political activities. As a result, his home served as a stopping-off place for other ex-felons, who often also were ex-addicts or friends of ex-addicts. Another key locator, who developed numerous contacts and referrals, was a publicly known ex-addict and a social scientist who was still involved with "the life."

When the snowball sampling method is used and participants in the study are enlisted to help find other potential respondents, they become de facto research assistants. Although all participants in the study may be asked to refer others, all of them cannot and should not be engaged to assist the research on a regular basis. The characteristics of study respondents differ, and so do their abilities to help with the research effort. In addition to the characteristics mentioned above, the most important factor to consider when selecting respondents to assist regularly in the research is the extent to which the person can be trusted to understand the goals of the research and present the project to others in an acceptable and serious manner. Respondent research assistants come to represent the project in the community, and it is important that the information they disperse be credible and compatible with the research effort. Knowledge about a project can and often does become distorted, and rumors can develop that may hinder or completely stymie the endeavor. For example, several people began to phone and drop by the project office to be interviewed. They all used as a reference the same man, a person who had taken it upon himself to make referrals to the study. All the people referred by this self-appointed assistant in one way or another did not meet the research criteria. Rejecting these people often was done only with great difficulty. Many of them became indignant when they were rejected because they felt they were qualified for the study. Consequently, a decision had to be made not to accept any respondents who used the name of the questionable locator; in a short time, the contacts stopped.

As the research continued, we also discovered that, from time to time, we had to train our respondent assistants. The training, sometimes very brief, simply entailed ensuring that they clearly understood the eligibility criteria for new respondents. In addition, as the research progressed, the respondent assistants had to be retrained as new research needs emerged—for example, the need to locate new kinds of respondents, or to be informed of the reasons why a particular chain was terminated prematurely.

In addition to their importance in generating a sample, the locators helped solve another important difficulty. This problem was an ethical one that emanated from the possible suspicions and consequences of staff members directly contacting individuals whose success in breaking the bond of opiate addiction was related to their ability to hide the facts about their pasts from such persons as employers. For many people, the fact of the past addiction's becoming known would have seriously jeopardized their current adjustment. A locator who was also a friend of a potential respondent could more easily overcome this problem; already existing personal ties would ease the way for an interview (see Henslin 1972). Locators also helped to temper suspicions about research staff members being connected with federal or state law enforcement agencies, which might obtain the information provided by respondents and use it in unwanted ways.

### Controlling the Kinds of Chains and Numbers of Cases in a Chain

The data needed in any exploratory research endeavor differ depending on the stage of the study. In our use of the chain-referral sampling method we found that we had to start different chains for different reasons during each stage of the research. At first, the data-gathering effort was purely exploratory; the aim simply was to get started. The beginning effort was akin to chumming techniques used by fishermen who scatter bait over an area of water in hopes of luring fish into it. Of course, at the study's start, we began by making contacts, wherever possible, with people already known to meet the research criteria. The study also was publicized in various ways. At this initial stage, respondents were interviewed as soon as they were located and became available.

As the research progressed, control over referral chains became more specific and was based on substantive considerations (see Broadhead 1983). Now the staff exercised control in an attempt to ensure that the sample(s) included an array of respondents that, in qualitative terms if not rigorous statistical ones, reflected what was thought to be the general characteristics of the population in question. The major concern at this point was that the sample include both men and women, that it be made up of persons from all social-class and racial backgrounds, and that it contain people from different geographic areas and occupations.

As the data gathering continued, the early interviews and the characteristics of the respondents were subjected to an ongoing analysis. The analysis, at this point, was done in part to direct and guide existing and future referral chains. The sampling was still substantive, but control now was more *selective* than it was earlier. For example, an analysis of the characteristics of the first twenty respondents showed that a large proportion of them were currently working in drug treatment programs. In order not to bias the sample with too many drug-abuse counselors, a decision was made to exclude from the study potential respondents who were employed in drug treatment unless they were of research interest for other reasons.

At the selective sampling stage the research effort is not as simple as it may appear. Depending on the particular focus of study, it may be extremely difficult to start referral chains that will yield certain kinds of respondents. In our study, in spite of excellent entrée into the various black communities in California, and in spite of the fact that the sample included some black male respondents, the concentrated efforts of project staff members (including a black research assistant) resulted in only a single interview with an untreated black female.

As data gathering and analysis progressed still further, various patterns began to be sorted out and conceptualized, and these conceptualizations provided the basis for future sampling. Now, control over the referral chains was not only selective but it also was based on *theoretical* considerations. For example, it was discovered that a major factor affecting the recovery process was the extent to which the person had become involved in the world of addiction to the exclusion of participation in other, conventional social worlds. A more, rather than less, focused immersion in the world of addiction appeared to be most extensive and dramatic with people who were addicted in situations where the drug was, among other things, relatively difficult to obtain and expensive to purchase. This analysis guided future sampling efforts toward possible comparison groups that might contain persons who were addicted in situations where opiates were more accessible and less costly. Thus, attempts were made to start referral chains in medical circles, among nurses and physicians.

The final effort in controlling the kinds of referral chains was made on the basis of *verificational* considerations alone. Once the analysis had been developed to the point where it came to terms adequately with the materials in question, some referral chains were continued and individual cases deliberately selected for the purpose of confirming various aspects of the analysis. In exploratory studies such as this one, where the project was obligated to collect a predetermined number of interviews, it was thought prudent to leave some of the interviews to the latter stages of the study, to be used only for verification purposes. (A more detailed discussion of both theoretical and verificational sampling can be found in Glaser 1978; Glaser and Strauss 1967.)

Another problem that must be addressed and controlled when using the chain-referral sampling method has to do with limiting the number of respondents within any subgroup in the sample. We continually asked ourselves: How many cases should be collected, and in what direction should the referral chains be guided? The answers to these questions were based on at least two considerations: (1) the representativeness of the sample; and (2) repetition of the data.

When constructing an empirical analysis of qualitative data, the incoming data should be analyzed on an ongoing basis. The analytic effort, as has been shown, was both substantive and theoretical. The substantive analysis of the kinds of respondents provided information on which to base decisions to limit the size of any subgroup in the sample. This analysis helped assure that the sample characteristics would at least broadly correspond with those thought to exist in the actual population. (This procedure, to some extent, resembles "quota sampling"; see Smith 1975.) For example, in our study a decision was made to limit the number of respondents in the sample who had been addicted while living in foreign countries. The reasoning behind this decision was simply to prevent the possibility of so misshaping the sample that it would unduly reflect the experiences of people addicted in countries where the legal restrictions might vary too greatly from those in the United States.

The number of cases provided through any one kind of referral chain was also limited as the data became repetitious. At this point, staff members felt confident that the possible variations extant in that particular subgroup had been exhausted.

In actuality, both criteria at times were compromised in the light of practical considerations. In certain instances, additional but nonessential interviews were conducted so as not to alienate or offend an enthusiastic respondent who could jeopardize the continuation of a referral chain.

**Pacing and Monitoring Chains and Data Quality**

As the work continued, we learned that we had to pace the speed at which referral chains were initiated and developed. It is important to make a distinction here between the natural evolution and dissipation of a referral chain as it builds and exhausts itself through a social network and the deliberate regulation of the speed with which new chains are started and moved along as interviews are completed. Certain social pressures combine and create a sense of urgency to rush the development of new contacts and the completion of interviews. One problem resulted from the nature of the method itself. Referrals have a tendency to be made in groups as knowledge of the research quickly spreads out from the original source. Often, staff members feared that if they did not immediately follow up a referral, the lead would cool and the contact would be lost. In projects such as this one, an additional source of pressure comes from trying to meet sample quotas promised a funding agency. Thus, a strong tendency developed to complete interviews as soon as possible, which resulted in serious problems, especially when a number of different snowballs were proceeding simultaneously. If the tendency had developed in an unrestrained manner, the inclination would have directly affected the characteristics of the entire sample, the resulting data, and thus the analysis. Consequently, it was necessary to pace the speed at which the sample developed so that, from time to time, its progression was stimulated, slowed, or stopped temporarily.

Monitoring the quality of data being collected certainly is not a problem unique to the use of chain-referral sampling. However, certain problems emerge when it is used in exploratory efforts when open-ended interviewing is employed. At any point in the research course there must be some certainty that the correct information is being gathered. The quality of the data can be affected by many factors, including a growing fatigue and disinterest among the interviewers or possible misunderstandings concerning precisely what should be explored and probed in each new interview. Whatever the reasons, the data afforded through the chain-referral sampling method should be monitored in a regular and systematic manner.

In this study the interviews were tape-recorded, and monitoring the quality of information that was being gathered presented some formidable problems. (See Appendix B for the interview guide.) This was particularly true when the actual monitoring was done only after the tapes had been transcribed into typescript. This created a long delay between the actual interview and an analysis of the materials it contained. Several times in the study, interviews were conducted at a faster rate than they could be transcribed (a problem of pacing), and a large backlog of untranscribed tapes accumulated. At one point in the project, seven interviewers were employed, and a large number of untranscribed tapes piled up. Consequently, the monitoring of data quality fell a few weeks behind. The research concern was that incorrect or poor-quality interviews were being collected; if this proved true, they would have to be excluded from the analysis. A strategy was developed to help prevent this from happening: A sort of debriefing session was conducted with the staff after each interview was completed. Debriefings were instructional, they served to monitor the kinds of materials being collected, and they allowed the interviewers to share their feelings and discuss any problems they might have encountered.

## Conclusion

Qualitative sociological researchers have often been criticized on the basis that their data-gathering techniques and methods of analysis are not clearly stated and explained. Or, when research methods are described, they are criticized for being too vague or unsystematic. Some of this criticism is well founded, and although an increasing amount of attention is now being given to qualitative methodological procedures and problems, much remains unstated and unanalyzed.

The particular methodological procedures, and the problems encountered and resolved in their use in the course of any study, to some degree reflect the singularities of the social phenomena being investigated (Becker 1970). A description and analysis of the problems and decisions made to overcome them in any single research endeavor would help to temper some of the criticism of qualitative sociology and increase its credibility with some audiences. In addition, the analysis of the qualitative methods as they are actually implemented and altered in research practice would provide the basis for possible future comparative analysis. An analysis of qualitative research methods as they have been used in different but substantively comparable sociological studies would likely yield more broad and systematic statements concerning qualitative methodological procedures than currently are available.

# Appendix B. Interview Guide for Tape-Recorded Sessions

What follows is the guide used in conducting the study interviews. The researchers were instructed to follow the guide as closely as possible:

In this section of the interview I would like you to tell me the story of how you overcame your addiction. Let's start by talking about the six-month period prior to your recovery. Could you begin by describing what brought about your decision to stop using drugs? Explore the following general areas:

- Life involvements, problems, extent of drug use, and self-conception prior to recovery
- Conditions that brought about idea to stop
- Actions taken to enact idea to stop
- Role that others played in giving rise to idea of stopping and the help they provided to realize the idea
- Various problems confronted and the ways they were handled in the process of maintaining resolve to stop
- Changes undergone in self-conception, lifestyle, and ideas about the future

Interviewer should probe the following specific areas as they apply.
1. Life involvements, extent of drug use, and self-conception prior to recovery.
   a. Relationships at the time (with family, with other drug users, with nonuser friends, etc.)
   b. Ability to support addiction

     *c.* Availability of drugs
     *d* Physical health (problems)
     *e.* Attitude toward self and addiction (e.g., did you feel positive or negative? strong willed or weak?)
     *f.* Personal troubles (e.g., did you have feelings of inadequacy, insecurity, or think of suicide?)
     *g.* Previous attempts to give up drugs
     *h.* Rock-bottom phenomenon (feelings of mortification and loss of meaning, having no one or nowhere to turn)
     *i.* Trouble with law
     *j.* Overdoses
     *k.* Death of friends
     *l.* Religious/spiritual conversion

2. Did any particular person or persons influence your decision to stop abusing drugs?
     *a.* Relationships with influential persons
     *b.* Kinds of influences they contributed

3. Specifically, what did you do to stop taking drugs?
     *a.* Specific actions
     *b.* Assistance sought
     *c.* Severity of withdrawal symptoms
     *d.* Second thoughts and ways they were handled
     *e.* Prior thoughts of stopping before actual attempt
     *f.* Willpower (e.g., how did you know, or what made you think, you could stop?)

4. After you kicked, did you have any urges (or cravings) to use opiates again?
     *a.* Specific coping mechanisms to handle urges or cravings
     *b.* Assistance given by others
     *c.* Kinds of temptations experienced and ways managed
     *d.* Cravings (e.g., how long did you experience them before you were comfortable? Did you backslide?)

5. How did you handle your drug-using friends when you were trying to stay off drugs?
     *a.* Geographic cure
     *b.* Leisure activities
     *c.* Social drug situations (e.g., going to a party and drugs are there)
     *d.* Establishing and maintaining relationships with straights

6. How did you handle your feelings? (Explore on day-to-day basis.)
   a. Ways handled anxiety states (when you felt uncomfortable or ill at ease, situations where you felt you didn't fit—restaurants, banks, etc.)
   b. Ways handled personal crises (e.g., when you felt put down, a failure, or couldn't pay your bills)
   c. Probe for psychological state of crisis—feelings of lethargy, morbidity, dread, etc.

7. How did you go about developing a new lifestyle?
   a. New daily routines
   b. Avoiding old hangouts
   c. New work
   d. New interests
   e. New hobbies
   f. New friends
   g. New old lady (old man) or spouse

8. I would like to get an idea of what your life is like now. Could you tell me what you did on a typical day last week, for example on Wednesday? (Go over the whole day from time got up to bedtime.)

9. What, if anything, took the place of drugs and the drug lifestyle in your life?
   a. Religion
   b. Ideologies
   c. Political activities
   d. Work/career
   e. Shifts in values
   f. Interest in money, marriage, family, etc.
   g. Helping other people
   h. Other drugs—alcohol, etc.
   i. Education

10. How would you describe your new lifestyle?
    a. Whom do you live with (are they really different from others)?
    b. How did you spend your money last month?
    c. Who are your close friends (what do they do)?
    d. What are your important new values?

11. How does your present lifestyle differ from your old lifestyle?

12. What are your plans for the future?
    *a.* Plans for next year
    *b.* Plans for next five years
    *c.* Plans for purchases or things to do (e.g., travel)

13. Who, among the people you now know well, knows that you are an ex-addict?
    *a.* Employer
    *b.* People you work with
    *c.* Good friends
    *d.* People in the neighborhood
    *e.* Relatives

14. How do people who knew you when you were addicted treat you now?
    *a.* Spouse and/or family
    *b.* Old friends
    *c.* People in the neighborhood

15. What difficulties have you experienced since giving up your old lifestyle?
    *a.* Job
    *b.* Housing
    *c.* Finances
    *d.* Work
    *e.* New friends
    *f.* Women/men

16. What are your achievements since changing life? (Where are efforts being channeled?)
    *a.* Material objects (clothes, home, etc.)
    *b.* Health (physical and mental)
    *c.* Success at work
    *d.* Relationships
    *e.* Family
    *f.* Travel
    *g.* New experiences
    *h.* New leisure
    *i.* Causes (e.g., politics)
    *j.* Acquiring money or security
    *k.* Education

17. What are your attitudes toward the conception of addiction and drug treatment?
    *a.* Explanation of addiction?

    *b.* Acceptance or rejection of addict, "dope fiend" labels (past and present)?

    *c.* Responsibility for actions versus forces in the environment (personal philosophy)?

    *d.* Getting help from institutionalized treatment or not?

18. Have you noticed any changes in your mental outlook since you stopped or curtailed your drug abuse?

    *a.* Toward family

    *b.* Toward community/friends

    *c.* Toward society

    *d.* Toward other drug users

    *e.* Toward work

    *f.* Toward the law/police

    *g.* Toward religion

19. How, if at all, have other people helped you maintain your decision not to use opiates?

20. Could you please summarize what you believe were the most *important things that led to your present lifestyle? And the most significant things that have helped you to control your drug use?*

# Appendix C. Characteristics of Individual Respondents

## Major Characteristics

| Case Number | Sex | Race[a] | Age at Interview | Primary Addicting Opiate | Years Addicted | Years Since Last Addiction | Age When Stopped |
|---|---|---|---|---|---|---|---|
| 001 | M | White | 33 | Heroin & Dilaudid | 1 | 5 | 28 |
| 002 | M | White | 36 | Morphine | 1 | 10 | 26 |
| 003 | M | White | 40 | Heroin | 4 | 16 | 34 |
| 004 | F | White | 29 | Heroin | 4 | 9 | 20 |
| 005 | F | Chicana Am. Indian | 32 | Heroin | 7 | 3 | 29 |
| 006 | M | White | 31 | Heroin | 5 | 3 | 28 |
| 007 | M | Black-Chicano | 46 | Heroin | 2 | 5 | 41 |
| 008 | F | Chicana | 31 | Heroin | 3 | 10 | 21 |
| 009 | M | White | 27 | Heroin | 1 + 6 mo. | 5 | 22 |
| 010 | M | White | 32 | Heroin | 5 | 8 | 24 |
| 011 | F | White | 37 | Heroin | 5 + 8 mo. | 13 | 24 |
| 012 | M | Chicano | 47 | Heroin | 4 + 5 mo. | 26 | 21 |
| 013 | F | Chicana | 26 | Heroin | 3 | 6 + 6 mo. | 19 + 6 mo. |
| 014 | M | Chicano | 32 | Heroin | 1 | 7 | 25 |
| 015 | F | White | 36 | Heroin | 4 | 15 + 7 mo. | 20 + 5 mo. |
| 016 | F | White | 25 | Heroin | 3 | 3 + 6 mo. | 21 + 6 mo. |
| 017 | M | White | 26 | Heroin | 3 | 3 | 23 |
| 018 | M | White | 39 | Heroin & Morphine | 5 | 7 | 32 |
| 019 | F | White | 20 | Heroin | 3 | 2 | 18 |
| 020 | F | White | 32 | Heroin | 2 + 6 mo. | 2 + 6 mo. | 29 + 6 mo. |
| 021 | M | White | 37 | Heroin | 3 | 12 | 25 |
| 022 | F | White | 26 | Heroin | 2 + 6 mo. | 3 | 23 |
| 023 | M | White | 29 | Heroin | 4 | 6 | 23 |
| 024 | M | Black | 49 | Heroin | 15 | 7 | 42 |
| 025 | M | White | 46 | Heroin | 2 | 11 | 35 |
| 026 | M | Black | 28 | Heroin | 2 + 6 mo. | 3 | 25 |

# Major Characteristics—Continued

| Case Number | Sex | Race[a] | Age at Interview | Primary Addicting Opiate | Years Addicted | Years Since Last Addiction | Age When Stopped |
|---|---|---|---|---|---|---|---|
| 027 | F | White | 37 | Heroin | 3 | 11 | 26 |
| 028 | M | White | 33 | Heroin & Morphine | 5 | 6 | 27 |
| 029 | M | Chicano | 23 | Heroin | 1 + 6 mo. | 3 | 20 |
| 030 | M | White | 38 | Dilaudid | 1 | 18 | 20 |
| 031 | F | White | 29 | Heroin | 4 | 5 | 24 |
| 032 | M | White | 36 | Heroin | 3 | 9 | 27 |
| 033 | M | White | 29 | Heroin | 5 | 2 | 27 |
| 034 | F | White | 29 | Heroin | 5 | 2 | 27 |
| 035 | M | White | 30 | Heroin | 12 | 5 | 25 |
| 036 | M | White | 29 | Heroin | 4 | 5 | 24 |
| 037 | M | Chicano | 40 | Heroin | 6 | 20 | 20 |
| 038 | M | Chicano | 55 | Heroin | 30 | 3 | 52 |
| 039 | M | White | 31 | Heroin | 3 | 7 | 34 |
| 040 | M | Latino | 41 | Heroin | 23 | 6 | 35 |
| 041 | M | Chicano | 30 | Heroin | 7 | 7 | 23 |
| 042 | M | Black | 26 | Heroin | 2 | 4 | 22 |
| 043 | M | Chicano | 52 | Heroin | 23 + 6 mo. | 12 | 40 |
| 044 | M | Chicano | 28 | Heroin | 1 + 6 mo. | 3 | 25 |
| 045 | M | Black | 39 | Heroin | 3 + 6 mo. | 8 | 31 |
| 046 | M | Black | 54 | Heroin & Morphine | 24 | 5 | 49 |
| 047 | M | Black | 27 | Heroin | 5 | 7 | 20 |
| 048 | F | White | 24 | Heroin | 3 | 6 | 18 |
| 049 | F | White | 31 | Heroin | 3 | 6 | 25 |
| 050 | M | Black | 34 | Heroin | 2 | 12 | 22 |
| 051 | M | Black | 36 | Heroin | 1 + 6 mo. | 8 | 28 |
| 052 | M | Black | 43 | Heroin | 6 | 6 | 37 |
| 053 | M | Chicano | 50 | Heroin | 21 | 7 + 7 mo. | 42 + 5 mo. |
| 054 | M | Black | 30 | Heroin | 1 + 10 mo. | 4 + 6 mo. | 25 + 6 mo. |
| 055 | M | White | 31 | Heroin | 5 | 3 | 28 |
| 056 | F | White | 30 | Heroin | 1 + 6 mo. | 7 | 23 |
| 057 | M | White | 27 | Heroin | 7 | 3 | 24 |
| 058 | F | White | 23 | Heroin | 7 | 3 | 20 |
| 059 | F | White | 25 | Heroin | 2 + 5 mo. | 4 + 10 mo. | 20 + 2 mo. |
| 060 | M | Chicano | 25 | Heroin | 4 | 3 + 5 mo. | 21 + 7 mo. |
| 061 | F | Black | 38 | Heroin | 3 | 2 + 6 mo. | 35 + 6 mo. |
| 062 | M | White | 29 | Heroin | 8 | 4 | 25 |
| 063 | M | White | 32 | Heroin | 1 + 6 mo. | 4 | 28 |
| 064 | F | White | 27 | Heroin | 10 | 2 | 25 |
| 065 | F | White | 42 | Heroin | 2 | 5 | 37 |
| 066 | M | White | 39 | Heroin | 2 + 6 mo. | 2 | 37 |
| 067 | M | Chicano | 35 | Heroin | 6 | 6 | 29 |

## Major Characteristics—Continued

| Case Number | Sex | Race[a] | Age at Interview | Primary Addicting Opiate | Years Addicted | Years Since Last Addiction | Age When Stopped |
|---|---|---|---|---|---|---|---|
| 068 | M | White | 39 | Heroin | 6 | 14 | 25 |
| 069 | M | White | 34 | Heroin | 9 | 4 | 30 |
| 070 | M | White | 20 | Heroin | 2 | 3 | 17 |
| 071 | M | White | 42 | Heroin | 4 | 10 | 32 |
| 072 | M | White | 31 | Heroin | 13 | 2 | 29 |
| 073 | F | White | 28 | Heroin | 2 | 7 | 21 |
| 074 | M | White | 37 | Heroin | 2 + 6 mo. | 7 | 30 |
| 075 | M | White | 29 | Heroin | 1 | 8 + 9 mo. | 20 + 3 mo. |
| 076 | M | White | 35 | Heroin | 12 | 4 + 6 mo. | 30 + 6 mo. |
| 077 | F | White | 32 | Heroin | 3 | 2 + 3 mo. | 29 + 9 mo. |
| 078 | F | Creole/ White | 28 | Heroin | 3 | 7 | 21 |
| 079 | F | White | 40 | Heroin | 1 + 2 mo. | 20 | 20 |
| 080 | F | White | 34 | Heroin | 1 + 6 mo. | 8 | 26 |
| 081 | M | White | 28 | Opium | 5 | 2 + 6 mo. | 25 + 6 mo. |
| 082 | F | White | 30 | Heroin | 3 | 4 | 26 |
| 083 | M | White | 25 | Heroin | 5 | 4 | 21 |
| 084 | M | White | 29 | Heroin | 6 | 6 | 23 |
| 085 | M | White | 30 | Heroin | 3 | 4 | 26 |
| 086 | M | White | 31 | Heroin | 3 | 6 + 3 mo. | 24 + 8 mo. |
| 087 | M | White | 31 | Heroin | 3 | 3 + 6 mo. | 27 + 6 mo. |
| 088 | M | White | 32 | Heroin | 10 | 4 | 28 |
| 089 | M | White | 36 | Heroin | 20 | 2 | 34 |
| 090 | M | White | 46 | Heroin | 6 | 12 | 34 |
| 091 | M | White | 36 | Opium & Heroin | 17 | 6 | 30 |
| 092 | M | White | 31 | Heroin | 4 | 6 | 25 |
| 093 | M | Persian | 26 | Opium | 9 | 3 | 23 |
| 094 | F | White | 23 | Heroin | 1 + 6 mo. | 5 | 18 |
| 095 | M | White | 36 | Heroin | 7 | 6 + 6 mo. | 29 + 6 mo. |
| 096 | F | White | 23 | Heroin | 3 | 3 | 20 |
| 097 | M | White | 31 | Heroin | 10 | 2 + 6 mo. | 28 + 6 mo. |
| 098 | M | White | 29 | Heroin | 6 | 2 + 7 mo. | 26 + 5 mo. |
| 099 | M | White | 40 | Opium | 3 | 6 | 34 |
| 100 | M | White | 32 | Heroin | 6 | 4 | 28 |
| 101 | F | White | 35 | Heroin | 17 | 2 | 33 |
| Averages | | | 33.78 | | 5.69 | 5.97 | 26.99 |

[a] Race was determined on the basis of self-identification.

# Respondent Characteristics: Summary Tables

## C1.  Age

|  | *No. of Cases* |
|---|---|
| 25 or less | 11 |
| 26–30 | 30 |
| 31–35 | 26 |
| 36–40 | 21 |
| 41–45 | 4 |
| 46–50 | 6 |
| 51 or more | 3 |
| Total | 101 |

## C2.  Sex

|  | *No. of Cases* |
|---|---|
| Male | 71 |
| Female | 30 |
| Total | 101 |

## C3.  Education

|  | *No. of Cases* |
|---|---|
| 8 years or less | 3 |
| 9–11 years | 13 |
| High school or GED | 26 |
| Some college/no degree | 38 |
| A.A. degree | 4 |
| B.A. degree | 8 |
| B.A.+ | 9 |
| Total | 101 |

## C4. Racial/Ethnic Background

|  | No. of Cases |
|---|---|
| Black | 12 |
| Chicano/Latino | 14 |
| White | 72 |
| Other (e.g., American Indian, Creole/White) | 3 |
| Total | 101 |

## C5. Area Where Respondents Were Raised

|  | No. of Cases |
|---|---|
| San Francisco Bay | 12 |
| Los Angeles | 17 |
| Other California | 10 |
| Western U.S. | 6 |
| Southwestern U.S. | 6 |
| Midwestern U.S. | 15 |
| Eastern U.S. | 22 |
| Southeastern U.S. | 7 |
| Outside U.S. | 6 |
| Total | 101 |

## C6. Religion of Family

|  | No. of Cases |
|---|---|
| Baptist | 10 |
| Catholic | 42 |
| Fundamental Protestant (e.g., Pentecostal) | 3 |
| Jewish | 6 |
| Methodist, Presbyterian, Espicopalian | 17 |
| Other | 9 |
| None | 14 |
| Total | 101 |

**C7.  Reported Years of Addiction** [a]

|  | No. of Cases |
| --- | --- |
| 1–2 | 28 |
| 3–4 | 31 |
| 5–6 | 19 |
| 7–8 | 6 |
| 9–10 | 5 |
| 11–12 | 2 |
| 13–14 | 1 |
| 15 or more | 9 |
| Total | 101 |

[a]Length calculated from point of first addiction to last; includes voluntary and involuntary periods of abstinence.

**C8.  Years since Last Addiction**

|  | No. of Cases |
| --- | --- |
| 2 | 14 |
| 3–4 | 29 |
| 5–6 | 23 |
| 7–8 | 16 |
| 9–10 | 5 |
| 11–12 | 6 |
| 13–14 | 2 |
| 15 or more | 6 |
| Total | 101 |

**C9.  Reported Method Used to Support Addiction**

|  | No. of Cases |
| --- | --- |
| Mostly work | 21 |
| Mostly illegal | 46 |
| Half-work and half-illegal | 23 |
| No illegal activities | 3 |
| Other (e.g., supported by others) | 8 |
| Total | 101 |

### C10. Reported Arrests Before Stopping Addiction

| No. of Arrests | No. of Cases |
|---|---|
| 1–2 | 12 |
| 3–4 | 22 |
| 5–6 | 7 |
| 7–8 | 6 |
| 9–10 | 2 |
| 11–12 | 5 |
| 13–14 | 3 |
| 15 or more | 15 |
| No arrests/no answer | 29 |
| Total | 101 |

### C11. Reported Convictions

| No. of Convictions | No. of Cases |
|---|---|
| 1 | 17 |
| 2 | 10 |
| 3 | 8 |
| 4 | 6 |
| 5 | 6 |
| 6 | 3 |
| 7 | 3 |
| 8 | 1 |
| 9 or more | 9 |
| None | 38 |
| Total | 101 |

# References

Agar, Michael. *Ripping and Running*. New York: Seminar Press, 1973.

Agar, Michael, and Harvey Feldman. "A Four-City Study of PCP Users." In *Ethnography: A Research Tool for Policymakers in the Drug and Alcohol Fields*, edited by Carl Akins and George Beschner. Rockville, Md.: U.S. Department of Health and Human Services, 1980.

Akins, Carl, and George Beschner. *Ethnography: A Research Tool for Policymakers in the Drug and Alcohol Fields*. Rockville, Md.: National Institute on Drug Abuse, 1980.

Alexander, Bruce, and Patricia F. Hadaway, "Theories of Opiate Addiction: A Time for Pruning?" *Journal of Drug Issues* 11 (1981): 77–92.

Baba, Ali, as told to Edward Rose. *The Last Connection: A Story About Heroin*. Boulder, Colo.: Waiting Room Press, 1980.

Becker, Howard S. "Notes on the Concept of Commitment." *American Journal of Sociology* 66 (1960): 32–40.

———. *Outsiders: Studies in the Sociology of Deviance*. New York: Free Press, 1963.

———. "The Self and Adult Socialization." In *The Study of Personality*, edited by Edward Norbeck, Douglass Price-Williams, and William McCord. New York: Holt, Rinehart and Winston, 1968.

———. "Practitioners of Vice and Crime." In *Pathways to Data*, edited by Robert Haberstein. Chicago: Aldine, 1970.

Berger, Peter, and Thomas Luckmann. *The Social Construction of Reality*. Garden City, N.Y.: Doubleday, 1966.

Bess, Barbara, Samuel Janus, and Alfred Rifkin. "Factors in Successful Narcotics Renunciation." *American Journal of Psychiatry* 128 (1972): 861–865.

Biernacki, Patrick. "Junkie Work, 'Hustles' and Social Status Among Heroin Addicts." *Journal of Drug Issues* 9 (1979): 535–551.

Biernacki, Patrick, and Fred Davis. "Turning Off: A Study of Ex-Marijuana Users." Paper presented at the Conference on Drug Use and Subcultures, Asilomar, California, 1970. Mimeo.

Biernacki, Patrick, and Dan Waldorf. "Snowball Sampling: Problems and Techniques of Chain Referral Sampling." *Sociological Methods and Research* 10 (1981): 141–163.

Blum, Richard H. "Drugs, Dangerous Behavior, and Social Policy." In *Task Force on Narcotics and Drug Abuse*. Prepared for the President's Commission on Law Enforcement and Administration of Justice. Washington, D.C.: Government Printing Office, 1967.

Blumer, Herbert. *Symbolic Interactionism: Perspective and Method.* Englewood Cliffs, N.J.: Prentice-Hall, 1969.

Brecher, Edward, and the Editors of Consumer Reports. *Licit and Illicit Drugs.* Boston: Little, Brown, 1972.

Brill, Leonard. *The De-Addiction Process.* Springfield, Ill.: Charles C Thomas, 1972.

Broadhead, Robert. *The Private Lives and Professional Identity of Medical Students.* New Brunswick, N.J.: Transaction Books, 1983.

Brotman, Richard, and Alfred Freedman. *A Community Mental Health Approach to Drug Addiction.* Washington, D.C.: Government Printing Office, 1968.

Burke, Kenneth. *Permanence and Change.* Indianapolis: Bobbs-Merrill, 1954.

Casriel, Daniel, and Grover Amen. *Daytop.* New York: Hill & Wang, 1971.

Charmaz, Kathy. "The Development of a Supernormal Identity in the Chronically Ill." Sonoma State University, Rohnert Park, California, 1981. Mimeo.

Chein, Isidor, and Eva Rosenfeld. "Juvenile Narcotic Use." *Law and Contemporary Problems* 22 (1957): 52–68.

Chein, Isidor, et al. *The Road to H.* New York: Basic Books, 1964.

Clinard, Marshall B. *Anomie and Deviant Behavior: A Discussion and Critique.* New York: Free Press, 1964.

Cloward, Richard A., and Lloyd E. Ohlin. *Delinquency and Opportunity: A Theory of Delinquent Gangs.* New York: Free Press, 1960.

Cochlin, J. "Factors Influencing Tolerance To and Dependence On

Narcotic Analgesics." In *Opiate Addiction: Origins and Treatment*, edited by S. Fisher and A. M. Freedman. Washington, D.C.: Winston, 1974.

Coleman, James W. "A Theory of Narcotics Abstinence." Paper presented at the annual meeting of the Society for the Study of Social Problems, San Francisco, 1978.

Denzin, Norman. *The Research Act*. New York: Free Press, 1970.

Dole, Vincent P. "Biochemistry of Addiction." *Annual Review of Biochemistry* 39 (1970): 821–840.

Dole, Vincent P., and Marie Nyswander. "Heroin Addiction—A Metabolic Disease." *Archives of Internal Medicine* 120 (1967): 19–24.

Dole, Vincent P., Marie Nyswander, and Alan Warner. "Successful Treatment of 750 Criminal Addicts." *Journal of American Medical Association* 206 (1968): 2708–2711.

Douglas, Jack. *Investigative Social Research: Individual and Team Research*. Beverly Hills, Calif.: Sage, 1976.

Duvall, Henrietta, Ben Locke, and Leon Brill. "Follow-up Study of Narcotic Drug Addicts After Hospitalization." *Public Health Reports* 78 (1963): 185–193.

Eistadter, Werner J. "The Social Organization of Armed Robbery." *Social Problems* 17 (1969): 64–83.

Feldman, Harvey. "Street Status Among Drug Users." *Society* 10 (1973): 32–38.

Gergen, Kenneth. *The Concept of Self*. New York: Holt, Rinehart and Winston, 1971.

———. "Multiple Identity: The Healthy, Happy Human Being Wears Many Masks." *Psychology Today*, 1972, 39–44.

Gerstein, Dean R. "Heroin in Motion: A Working Paper in the Theory of Action." Ph.D. dissertation, Harvard University, Cambridge, 1975.

Glaser, Barney. *Theoretical Sensitivity: Advances in the Methodology of Grounded Theory*. Mill Valley, Calif.: Sociology Press, 1978.

Glaser, Barney, and Anselm Strauss. *The Discovery of Grounded Theory: Strategies for Qualitative Research*. Chicago: Aldine, 1967.

Goffman, Erving. *Stigma: Notes on the Management of Spoiled Identity*. Englewood Cliffs, N.J.: Prentice-Hall, 1963.

Goldstein, A. "Heroin Addiction: Sequential Treatment Employing

Pharmacologic Supports." *Archives of General Psychiatry* 83 (1976): 353–358.

Graeven, David, and Kathleen Graeven. "Treated and Untreated Addicts: Factors Associated with Participation in Treatment and Cessation of Heroin Use." *Journal of Drug Issues* 13 (1983): 207–218.

Greenberg, Stephanie W., and Freda Adler. "Crime and Addiction: An Empirical Analysis of the Literature. 1920–1973." *Contemporary Drug Problems* 3 (1974): 221–270.

Hawkins, J. David, and Norman Wacker. "Verbal Performances and Addict Conversation: An Interactionist Perspective on Therapeutic Communities." *Journal of Drug Issues* 13 (1983): 281–298.

Henslin, James M. "Studying Deviance in Four Settings: Research Experiences with Cabbies, Suicides, Drug Users and Abortionees." In *Research on Deviance*, edited by Jack Douglas. New York: Random House, 1972.

Hewitt, John P. *Self and Society.* 2d ed. Boston: Allyn and Bacon, 1979.

Hochschild, Arlie Russell. "The Sociology of Feeling and Emotion." In *Another Voice*, edited by Marcia Millman and Rosabeth Moss Kanter. Garden City, N.Y.: Doubleday, 1975.

Hughes, Patrick H., et al. "The Social Structure of a Heroin Copping Community." *American Journal of Psychiatry* 128 (1971): 551–558.

Hunt, Dana E., et al. *It Takes Your Heart: The Image of Methadone Maintenance in the Addict World and Its Effects on Recruitment into Treatment.* New York: New York State Division of Substance Abuse Services, n.d.

Hunt, G. H., and M. E. Odoroff, "Follow-Up Study of Narcotic Drug Addicts After Hospitalization." *Public Health Reports* 17 (1962): 41–53.

Isbell, Harris, "Craving for Alcohol." *Quarterly Journal of Studies of Alcohol* 16 (1955): 34–64.

Jaffe, Jerome. "Narcotic Analgesics" and "Drug Addiction and Drug Abuse." In *The Pharmacological Basis of Therapeutics*, edited by Louis Goodman and Alfred Gilman. 4th ed. New York: Macmillan, 1970.

———. "Evaluating Drug Abuse Treatment: A Comment on the State of the Art." In *Drug Abuse Treatment Evaluation:*

*Strategies, Progress and Prospects.*, edited by Frank Tims and Jacqueline Ludford. Research Monograph no. 51. Rockville, Md.: U.S. Department of Health and Human Services, 1983.

Jones, H. *Sensual Drugs.* Cambridge, England: Cambridge University Press, 1977.

Jorquez, James. "The Retirement Phase of Heroin Using Careers." *Journal of Drug Issues* 13 (1983): 343–366.

Knupfer, G. "Ex-Problem Drinkers." In *Life History Research in Psychopathology*, vol. 2, edited by M. Roff, L. Robins, and H. Pollack. Minneapolis: University of Minnesota Press, 1972.

Kramer, John. "From Demon to Ally—How Mythology Has, and May Yet, Alter National Drug Policy." *Journal of Drug Issues* 6 (1976): 390–406.

Lemert, Edwin. "An Isolation and Closure Theory of Naive Check Forgery." *Journal of Criminal Law, Criminology and Police Science* 44 (1953): 296–307.

———. *Human Deviance, Social Problems and Social Control.* Englewood Cliffs, N.J.: Prentice-Hall, 1967.

Lewis, Virginia, and Daniel Glaser. "Lifestyles Among Heroin Users." *Federal Probation* 38 (1974): 21–28.

Lindesmith, Alfred. *Addiction and Opiates.* Chicago: Aldine, 1968.

Lindesmith, Alfred, Anselm Strauss, and Norman Denzin. *Social Psychology.* 4th ed. Hinsdale, Ill.: Dryden Press, 1975.

Lofland, John. *Deviance and Identity.* Englewood Cliffs, N.J.: Prentice-Hall, 1969.

McAuliffe, William. "A Test of Wikler's Theory of Relapse: The Frequency of Relapse Due to Conditioned Withdrawal Sickness." *International Journal of the Addictions* (forthcoming).

McAuliffe, William, and Robert Gordon. "A Test of Lindesmith's Theory of Addiction: The Frequency of Euphoria Among Long-Term Addicts." *American Journal of Sociology* 79 (1974): 795–840.

———. "Reinforcement and the Combination of Effects: A Social-Psychological Theory of Opiate Addicts." In *Theories of Addiction*, edited by Dan Lettieri. Washington, D.C.: National Institute on Drug Abuse, 1981.

Maddux, James, and David P. Desmond. "New Light on the Maturing Out Hypotheses in Opiad Dependence." Department of Psychiatry, University of Texas Health Science Center, San Antonio, 1979. Mimeo.

Mahoney, M. J. *Cognitive and Behavior Modification.* Cambridge, Mass.: Bollinger, 1974.

Marris, Peter, and Martin Rein. *Dilemmas of Social Reform.* 2d ed. Chicago: Aldine, 1967.

Martin, W. R. "The Basis and Possible Utility of the Use of Opioid Antagonists in the Ambulatory Treatment of the Addict." In *Addictive States,* edited by A. Wikler. Baltimore: Williams and Wilkins, 1968.

Martin, W. R., and H. F. Fraser. "Comparative Study of the Physiological and Subjective Effects of Heroin and Morphine Administered Intravenously in Post-Addicts." *Journal of Pharmacology and Experimental Therapeutics* 133 (1961): 389–399.

Mead, George Herbert. *Mind, Self and Society.* Chicago: University of Chicago Press, 1934.

Merton, Robert K. *Social Theory and Social Structure.* Enlarged ed. New York: Free Press, 1957.

Movahedi, Siamak. "The Drug Addict and Addiction: Cultural Stereotypes and Clinical Theories." *Urban Life* 7 (1978): 45–67.

Moynihan, Daniel P. *Maximum Feasible Misunderstanding.* New York: Free Press, 1969.

Musto, David. *The American Disease.* New Haven: Yale University Press, 1973.

Nelkin, Dorothy. *Methadone Maintenance: A Technological Fix.* New York: Braziller, 1973.

O'Donnell, John A., et al. *Young Men and Drugs: A Nationwide Survey.* NIDA research monograph. Washington, D.C.: U.S. Department of Health and Human Services, 1976.

Platt, Jerome, and Christine Labate. *Heroin Addiction: Theory, Research and Treatment.* New York: Wiley, 1976.

Preble, Edward, and John Casey. "Taking Care of Business: The Heroin User's Life on the Streets." *International Journal of the Addictions* 4 (1969): 1–24.

*Proceedings of the Institute on Narcotic Addiction Among Mexican Americans in the Southwest* Publication No. (H5M) 73–9085. Washington, D.C.: U.S. Department of Health, Education, and Welfare, 1973.

Rado, Sandor. "The Psychoanalysis of Pharmacothymia (Drug Addiction)." *Psychoanalytic Quarterly* 2 (1933): 1–23.

Ray, Marsh, "The Cycle of Abstinence and Relapse Among Heroin Addicts." *Social Problems* 9 (1961): 132–140.

Ray, Oakley. *Drugs, Society and Human Behavior.* 2d ed. St. Louis: Mosby, 1978.

Restak, Richard. "The Brain Makes Its Own Narcotics." *Science Review* 35 (1977): 7–11.

Robins, Lee N. *The Vietnam Drug User Returns.* Washington, D.C.: Government Printing Office, 1973.

Rosenbaum, Marsha. "Funneling Options: The Career of the Woman Addict." Ph.D. dissertation, Graduate Program in Sociology, University of California Medical Center, San Francisco, 1979.

Rubington, Earl. "The Natural History of Sober Careers." Department of Sociology and Anthropology, Northeastern University, Boston, 1978. Mimeo.

Scharse, Robert. "Cessation Patterns Among Neophyte Heroin Users." *International Journal of the Addictions* 1 (1966): 23–32.

Schur, Edwin M. *Crimes Without Victims: Deviant Behavior and Public Policy.* Englewood Cliffs, N.J.: Prentice-Hall, 1965.

Senay, Edward. "Clinical Implications of Drug Abuse Treatment Outcome Research." In *Drug Abuse Treatment Evaluation: Strategies, Programs and Prospects,* edited by Frank Tims and Jacqueline Ludford. NIDA Research Monograph no. 51. Rockville, Md.: U.S. Department of Health and Human Services, 1983.

Simpson, D. Dwayne. "National Treatment System Evaluation Based on the Drug Abuse Reporting System (DARP) Follow-up Research." In *Drug Abuse Treatment Evaluation: Strategies, Progress and Prospects,* edited by Frank Tims and Jacqueline Ludford. NIDA Research Monograph no. 51. Rockville, Md.: U.S. Department of Health and Human Services, 1983.

Smith, H. W. *Strategies of Social Research: The Sociological Imagination.* Englewood Cliffs, N.J.: Prentice-Hall, 1975.

Snyder, S. H. "Opiate Receptors in the Brain." *New England Journal of Medicine* 296 (1977): 266–271.

Stall, Ronald D. "An Examination of Spontaneous Remission from Problem Drinking in the Bluegrass Region of Kentucky." *Journal of Drug Issues* 13 (1983): 191–206.

Stall, Ronald D., and Patrick Biernacki. "Spontaneous Remission from the Problematic Use of Substances." *International Journal of the Addictions* (1986).

Stephens, Richard, and Emily Cottrell. "A Follow-Up Study of 200 Narcotic Addicts Committed for Treatment Under the Narcotics Rehabilitation Act (NARA)." *British Journal of Addictions* 67 (1972): 45–63.

Stimson, Gerry V. *Heroin and Behavior.* New York: Wiley, 1974.

Strauss, Anselm. "A Social World Perspective." *Studies in Symbolic Interaction* 1 (1978): 119–128.

Sutter, Allan. "The World of the Righteous Dope Fiend." *Issues in Criminology* 2 (1966): 177–182.

Taylor, J. R., and Larry Lantinga. "Urge Reduction Training: A Behavior Therapy Strategy for Substance Abusers." University of Utah, Salt Lake City, 1979. Mimeo.

Tuchfeld, Barry S. "Spontaneous Remission in Alcoholics: Empirical Observations and Theoretical Implications." *Journal of Studies on Alcohol* 42 (1981): 626–641.

Tuchfeld, Barry S., et al. *Changes in the Patterns of Alcohol Use Without the Aid of Formal Treatment: An Exploratory Study of Former Drinkers.* Research Triangle Park, N.C.: Research Triangle Institute, 1976.

Volkman, Rita, and Donald Cressey. "Differential Association and the Rehabilitation of Drug Addicts." *American Journal of Sociology* 69 (1963): 129–142.

Waldorf, Dan. "Natural Recovery from Opiate Addiction: Some Social–Psychological Processes of Untreated Recovery." *Journal of Drug Issues* 13, no. 2 (Spring 1983): 237–280.

Waldorf, Dan, and Patrick Biernacki. "Natural Recovery from Heroin Addiction: A Review of the Literature." *Journal of Drug Issues* 9 (1979): 281–289.

———. "The Natural Recovery from Opiate Addiction: Some Preliminary Findings." *Journal of Drug Issues* 11, no. 1 (Winter 1981): 61–76.

Webb, Eugene J., et al. *Unobtrusive Measures: Nonreactive Research in the Social Sciences.* Chicago: Rand McNally, 1966.

Wikler, Abraham. *Opiate Addiction.* Springfield, Ill.: Charles C Thomas, 1953.

———. "Conditioning Factors in Opiate Addiction and Relapse." In *Narcotics,* edited by D. M. Wilmer and G. G. Kassebaum. New York: McGraw-Hill, 1965.

————. "Dynamics of Drug Dependence: Implications of a Conditioning Theory for Research and Treatment." *Archives of General Psychiatry* 28 (1973): 611–616.

Winick, Charles. "Maturing Out of Narcotic Addiction." *Bulletin on Narcotics* 14 (1962): 1–7.

Yablonsky, Lewis. *Synanon: The Tunnel Back.* New York: Macmillan, 1965.

Zinberg, Norman, and Wayne Harding. "Control and Intoxication Use: A Theoretical and Practical Overview." *Journal of Drug Issues* 9 (1979): 121–144.

Zinberg, Norman, and Richard Jacobson. "The Natural History of 'Chipping.'" *American Journal of Psychiatry* 133 (1976): 37–40.

# Index